Hamlyn Kitchen Shelf

FAMILY
COOKING

Annette Wolter

Hamlyn
London · NewYork · Sydney · Toronto

This edition published by
The Hamlyn Publishing Group Limited
London · New York · Sydney · Toronto
Astronaut House, Feltham, Middlesex, England
© Copyright The Hamlyn Publishing Group Limited 1982

ISBN 0 600 32284 X

First published under the title
Gesunde Küche für jeden Tag
© Copyright by Gräfe und Unzer Verlag, München

Set in 10 on 11pt Monophoto Sabon 669
by Tameside Filmsetting Ltd,
Ashton-under-Lyne, Lancashire
Printed in Italy

Contents

Useful facts and figures

Notes on metrication

In this book quantities are given in metric and Imperial measures. Exact conversion from Imperial to metric measures does not usually give very convenient working quantities and so the metric measures have been rounded off into units of 25 grams. The table below shows the recommended equivalents.

Ounces	Approx g to nearest whole figure	Recommended conversion to nearest unit of 25
1	28	25
2	57	50
3	85	75
4	113	100
5	142	150
6	170	175
7	198	200
8	227	225
9	255	250
10	283	275
11	312	300
12	340	350
13	368	375
14	396	400
15	425	425
16 (1 lb)	454	450
17	482	475
18	510	500
19	539	550
20 ($1\frac{1}{4}$ lb)	567	575

Note: When converting quantities over 20 oz first add the appropriate figures in the centre column, then adjust to the nearest unit of 25. As a general guide, 1 kg (1000 g) equals 2.2 lb or about 2 lb 3 oz. This method of conversion give good results in nearly all cases, although in certain pastry and cake recipes a more accurate conversion is necessary to produce a balanced recipe.

Liquid measures The millilitre has been used in this book and the following table gives a few examples.

Imperial	Approx ml to nearest whole figure	Recommended ml
$\frac{1}{4}$ pint	142	150 ml
$\frac{1}{2}$ pint	283	300 ml
$\frac{3}{4}$ pint	425	450 ml
1 pint	567	600 ml
$1\frac{1}{2}$ pint	851	900 ml
$1\frac{3}{4}$ pints	992	1000 ml (1 litre)

Spoon measures All spoon measures given in this book are level unless otherwise stated.

Can sizes At present, cans are marked with the exact (usually to the nearest whole number) metric equivalent of the Imperial weight of the contents, so we have followed this practice when giving can sizes.

Oven temperatures

The table below gives recommended equivalents.

	°C	°F	Gas Mark
Very cool	110	225	$\frac{1}{4}$
	120	250	$\frac{1}{2}$
Cool	140	275	1
	150	300	2
Moderate	160	325	3
	180	350	4
Moderately hot	190	375	5
	200	400	6
Hot	220	425	7
	230	450	8
Very hot	240	475	9

Note: WHEN MAKING ANY OF THE RECIPES IN THIS BOOK, ONLY FOLLOW ONE SET OF MEASURES AS THEY ARE NOT INTERCHANGEABLE.

Introduction

One of the stiffest challenges to the housewife's ingenuity is the planning of the daily menu. 'What shall I give them for dinner?' is a heartfelt cry in many a household, where fresh ideas for tasty, interesting meals are more than welcome.

It is in this context that Annette Wolter has devised a book that is especially helpful to the family cook. Here in *Family Cooking* are time-saving dishes which can be quickly prepared; succulent joints, simple casseroles, vegetables and soups. Many of these recipes have a subtle, continental touch, for Annette Wolter has brought her German expertise to bear on the everyday dishes that we all know, adding a herb or a flavour that is slightly different, less familiar to us, but producing a dish that is even more delicious.

The range is wide: following a selection of appetising soups, there is a choice of fish recipes, making full use of the varieties of canned or frozen shellfish available, and a generous serving of mouth-watering meat dishes, each with its own rich sauce, touch of garnish or vegetable accompaniment to provide an element of surprise to the tried and familiar – ideas that are simple, yet subtly different. Besides some interesting chicken dishes, the poultry and game section includes one or two recipes for those lucky enough to live in an area where venison or an occasional hare may be obtained, and there are also some exciting suggestions for supper dishes and tempting snacks, including salads and savouries and refreshing milk cocktails.

Desserts, too, have been included, though in these days of readily available fresh fruit and ice creams less emphasis has been placed on this aspect of the meal, in recognition of the fact that today's cooks cannot afford to spend too much time concocting elaborate puddings for a generation whose tastes run to the savoury rather than to the sweet.

There is nothing absolute about the suggestions that have been given for accompaniments to many of these recipes. If you prefer rice to pasta, or potatoes to both, your own preference could well be the best guide. Perhaps you like your potatoes creamed rather than boiled; but if there is cream already in the recipe this may prove too rich a mixture and the suggestion offered may steer you towards a simpler choice.

Some ingredients freeze more easily than others and those recipes that are especially suitable for freezing are recommended accordingly. It is important, however, to remember that food that has been frozen must be thoroughly reheated to boiling point before serving, and not just warmed through. This ensures that any harmful organisms that may be lurking are totally destroyed.

Though it may be too much to hope that every recipe in a cookery book will become an instant favourite, in *Family Cooking* the range of imaginative dishes will add colour to the family's menus and the inventive skill of the author will bring a touch of magic to the simplest meal.

Note: Each recipe in this book will serve four people unless otherwise stated.

Tasty soups

Country-style chicken soup

(Illustrated on opposite page)

1 (1.5-kg/3¼-lb) chicken
25 g/1 oz pearl barley
3 leeks
¼ celery head
2 large carrots
1 bunch parsley
1 teaspoon salt
2 litres/3½ pints water
¼ teaspoon white pepper
pinch of dried sage
pinch of dried rosemary
1 red pepper
350 g/12 oz frozen peas

Clean the chicken inside and out. Cut the roots off the leeks and trim the leaves, discarding any damaged ones. Wash well and slice them thinly. Wash the celery carefully and chop it. Clean, scrape and slice the carrots; wash and chop the parsley. Add the salt to the water and bring to the boil. Place the chicken, barley, leeks, celery, carrots and parsley in the boiling water, add the pepper, sage and rosemary, then cover and cook for 2 hours over a low heat.

Take the cooked chicken from the pan, remove the flesh from the bones and dice. Replace the chicken meat and reheat. Halve the pepper, deseed, cut the flesh into strips and add it to the soup. Add the peas and cook for a further 15 minutes over a low heat. Adjust the seasoning before serving.

Country-style chicken soup makes a substantial main dish. Any left over can be frozen and used later as the basis for a chicken fricassée, or the stock can be used for another soup with the substitution of different vegetables and rice or vermicelli. It must be thoroughly reheated before serving.

Suitable for freezing

Cream of celery soup

1 head celery (about 500 g/generous 1 lb)
500 ml/17 fl oz chicken stock
20 g/¾ oz butter or margarine
1 tablespoon plain flour
250 ml/8 fl oz milk
pinch of celery salt
pinch each of salt and pepper
100 ml/4 fl oz single cream
1 egg yolk

Wash the celery well, including any leaves. Cut off the leaves and chop them, then leave them on one side to dry. Dice the celery stalks. Bring the stock to the boil, put in the diced celery, cover and cook until tender.

Liquidise the celery and stock in a blender. Melt the butter or margarine, stir in the flour and heat gently, gradually adding the milk and stirring all the time until it comes to the boil. Add in the celery purée, celery salt, salt and pepper, then cover and heat gently. Mix the cream and egg yolk together with 1 tablespoon of the hot soup and gradually add this mixture to the soup. Do not allow the soup to boil again or the egg will curdle. Adjust the seasoning and garnish with the chopped raw celery leaves.

Suitable for freezing: If the soup is to be frozen, do not add the cream and egg yolk mixture until after it has been thawed again and thoroughly reheated.

Curried cucumber soup

1 large cucumber
pinch of celery salt
1 teaspoon curry paste, or to taste
½ teaspoon salt
½ teaspoon castor sugar
750 ml/1¼ pints chicken stock
1 bunch fresh or 1 teaspoon dried chopped dill
150 ml/¼ pint soured cream

Peel and grate the cucumber. Mix with the celery salt, curry paste, salt and castor sugar and add to the stock. Cover, bring to the boil, then simmer gently for 5 minutes. Wash fresh dill, if used, pat dry with kitchen paper and chop. Take the soup off the heat, stir in the soured cream and sprinkle with dill before serving.

Cauliflower soup

1 large cauliflower (about 800 g/1¾ lb)
750 ml/1¼ pints chicken stock
150 ml/¼ pint single cream
pinch of grated nutmeg
salt and freshly ground pepper
4 tablespoons chopped parsley

Trim any coarse stalks from the cauliflower and cut into florets. Wash them thoroughly, then cook in boiling chicken stock to cover, until the florets are just tender. Mix together the cream, nutmeg salt and pepper. Liquidise in a blender the cooked cauliflower and stock, in two batches if necessary, then return the soup to the pan. Stir in the cream, cover and cook very gently for a further 5 minutes. Sprinkle with the chopped parsley and adjust the seasoning before serving.

Suitable for freezing: If the soup is to be frozen, it is best to freeze only the cauliflower purée and add the cream, seasoning and parsley when reheating the soup after thawing.

Country-style chicken soup

Pepper soup with cream

(Illustrated on opposite page)

2 green peppers
2 red peppers
3 onions
225 g/8 oz canned or bottled sauerkraut
3 tablespoons oil
1 tablespoon flour
1 litre/1¾ pints chicken stock
100 ml/4 fl oz single cream
4 tablespoons sweet white wine (optional)
salt and pepper
2 tablespoons chopped parsley

Wash and deseed the peppers and cut into strips, peel the onions and cut into rings. Separate the sauerkraut loosely with two forks. Heat the oil in a pan and fry the onion rings and pepper for a few minutes, stirring continuously, then add the sauerkraut and continue to cook. Sprinkle in the flour and cook for a minute, stirring constantly, then gradually add the stock and bring it to the boil. Cover and leave to simmer over a medium heat for 15 minutes. Stir in the cream, add the wine, season to taste and sprinkle with parsley.

Suitable for freezing: If the soup is to be frozen, do not add the cream and parsley until after it has been thawed again and reheated, then adjust the seasoning.

Cream of leek soup

500 g/1 lb leeks
25 g/1 oz butter or margarine
2 tablespoons plain flour
500 ml/17 fl oz chicken stock
200 ml/7 fl oz milk
pinch each of salt and pepper
pinch of grated nutmeg
2 tomatoes
4 tablespoons single cream

Cut off the roots and trim the leaves of the leeks, slice them in half lengthwise, wash thoroughly and finely slice. Melt the butter or margarine, add the leeks and cook gently until soft. Sprinkle in the flour and cook for a minute, stirring con-stantly, then gradually add the stock and milk and bring to the boil. Put in the leeks, add the salt, pepper and nutmeg, then cover and simmer for 20 minutes. Make a crosswise incision in the stalkless end of the tomatoes, cover with boiling water and leave for a minute. Peel the tomatoes, then cut into pieces discarding the seeds and add the flesh to the soup. Continue to cook for a little longer, then remove the soup from the heat, stir in the cream and adjust the seasoning.

Suitable for freezing: If the soup is to be frozen, do not add the cream until after the soup has been thawed and thoroughly reheated.

Cream of asparagus soup

500 g/1 lb asparagus, fresh or canned
750 ml/1¼ pints chicken stock
1 teaspoon sugar
40 g/1½ oz butter or margarine
2 tablespoons plain flour
2 egg yolks
generous pinch of pepper
generous pinch of saffron or turmeric (optional)
250 ml/8 fl oz single cream
4 tablespoons chopped parsley

Wash and trim the fresh asparagus, removing the woody part of the stem, and cut into 5-cm/2-inch pieces. Drain canned asparagus and cut in the same way. Bring the stock to the boil with the sugar, add the asparagus, cover and simmer over a medium heat for 20 minutes if asparagus is fresh, or 5 minutes if canned. Drain the asparagus and put aside.

Melt the butter or margarine in a pan, then add the flour and heat gently, stirring all the time, gradually adding the stock. Cover and continue to cook for a short time, then remove from the heat. Mix together the egg yolks, pepper, saffron or turmeric and cream, and stir into the soup. Return the asparagus to the soup, reheat, but do not allow to boil. Before serving, sprinkle with the parsley.

Suitable for freezing: If the soup is to be frozen, do not add the cream and egg yolks until after it has been thawed again and thoroughly reheated.

Pepper soup with cream

Spanish pea soup

750 ml/1¼ pints hot chicken stock
450 g/1 lb frozen peas
225 g/8 oz cooked ham
2 egg yolks
150 ml/¼ pint single cream
dash Worcestershire sauce
pinch each of salt and pepper
4 tablespoons chopped parsley

Put the stock in a pan, add the frozen peas, then bring to the boil. Cover the pan, lower the heat and cook gently for 6 minutes. Cut the ham into thin strips and add to the pan. Whisk the egg yolks with the cream, Worcestershire sauce, salt and pepper. Take the soup off the heat while you stir in the egg and cream mixture. Reheat, but do not allow it to boil. Sprinkle with parsley before serving.

French bean soup

350 g/12 oz French beans
1 onion
150 g/5 oz bacon, derinded
65 g/2½ oz butter or oil
2 tablespoons plain flour
1.25 litres/2¼ pints hot chicken stock
1 sprig savory (optional)
½ teaspoon salt
pinch of pepper
pinch of grated nutmeg
2 tablespoons single cream

Wash, trim and dice the beans. Peel and chop the onion and dice the bacon. Melt the butter or heat the oil in a pan and fry the onion and bacon. After a few minutes sprinkle on the flour, stirring constantly, cook for one minute, then gradually stir in the hot stock. Add the beans, savory and salt to the soup and sprinkle with pepper and grated nutmeg to taste. Bring the soup to the boil, then cover and simmer over a low heat for 30 minutes. Just before serving remove from the heat, stir in the cream and adjust the seasoning.

Sailor's special

575 g/1¼ lb cod fillets
1 onion
1 large carrot
40 g/1½ oz butter
2 tablespoons plain flour
750 ml/1¼ pints hot water
1 teaspoon salt
generous pinch dried tarragon
100 ml/4 fl oz dry white wine
150 g/5 oz shrimps or prawns, canned or frozen
1 (100-g/4-oz) can mussels
100 g/4 oz button mushrooms
4 tablespoons single cream
4 slices French bread

If frozen, allow the fish to thaw slightly at room temperature. Peel and chop the onion. Scrape and chop the carrot. Skin the fish and remove any bones, then cut into equal pieces with a sharp knife. Melt the butter in a pan, add the onion and carrot and fry for 5 minutes, stirring continuously. Sprinkle in the flour and cook for a minute, constantly stirring, then gradually add the hot water and bring to the boil. Put in the fish fillets, salt, tarragon and wine, cover and cook over a low heat for 15 minutes.

Drain the shrimps and mussels, wipe and slice the mushrooms, add them to the soup and continue to cook for a few more minutes. Just before serving, remove from the heat, stir in the cream and adjust the seasoning. Toast the bread and place a slice in each of four soup bowls, then pour on the soup.

Sailor's special

Poached fish with olive sauce

4 pieces cod or haddock (each weighing about 150 g/5 oz)
½ teaspoon salt
juice of ½ lemon
250 ml/8 fl oz white wine
250 ml/8 fl oz water
2 eggs
1 onion
225 g/8 oz mushrooms
20 stuffed green olives
2 tomatoes
1 clove garlic
3 tablespoons oil
pinch of allspice
pinch of dried oregano
pinch each of pepper and salt
2 tablespoons chopped parsley

Rinse and skin the fish pieces, pat dry and rub with salt and lemon juice. Bring the white wine and water to the boil in a pan, put in the fish, then cover and simmer gently for 15 minutes. Hard boil the eggs. Peel and chop the onion, wipe and slice the mushrooms and rinse, dry and chop the olives. Slit the tomatoes at one end, cover with boiling water and leave for a minute. Peel the tomatoes and finely chop, discarding the seeds. Peel and finely chop the garlic.

Heat the oil in a pan and fry the onion, stirring continuously. Add the mushrooms, olives, tomatoes and garlic and stir until well heated. Shell the eggs and chop them, mix with 350 ml/12 fl oz of the cooking liquid from the fish and add to the pan to make the sauce. Season with allspice, oregano, pepper and salt, then stir the sauce and allow to heat through gently for a few more minutes. Drain the fish and place on a warm dish, pour over the sauce and garnish with the parsley.

Serve with: Boiled potatoes or rice and green salad

Quick shrimp sauce

1 (200-g/7-oz) can shrimps or prawns
250 ml/8 fl oz milk or 125 ml/4 fl oz milk and 125 ml/4 fl oz single cream
250 ml/8 fl oz chicken stock
20 g/¾ oz butter or margarine
2 tablespoons plain flour
2 tablespoons white wine
pinch each of salt and pepper
pinch of grated nutmeg

Drain and separate the shrimps or prawns. Stir the milk into the chicken stock. Melt the butter or margarine in a pan, add the flour and, stirring all the time, cook for a minute over a low heat, then gradually add the milk and stock mixture and the wine and bring to the boil, stirring continuously. Season the sauce with salt, pepper and nutmeg and add the shrimps. Continue to heat for a few minutes without letting it boil.

To make a richer sauce, substitute single cream for half the quantity of milk, stirring it in after thickening the sauce and before adding the seasoning and shrimps.

Serve with: Cooked fish, chicken or vegetables

Quick shrimp cocktail

1 (200-g/7-oz) can shrimps or prawns
1 (280-g/10-oz) can asparagus spears
1 (280-g/10-oz) can mushrooms
2 tablespoons mayonnaise
4 tablespoons single cream
3 tablespoons tomato ketchup
pinch each of salt and pepper
pinch of paprika pepper
dash Worcestershire sauce
5 drops Tabasco sauce
1 tablespoon dry sherry
4 thin slices lemon, unpeeled

Drain and separate the shrimps or prawns. Drain the asparagus spears and mushrooms. Stir together the mayonnaise, cream, tomato ketchup, salt, pepper, paprika, Worcestershire sauce, Tabasco sauce and the sherry, then mix with the shrimps, asparagus and mushrooms. Divide the mixture between four glass bowls and garnish each with a slice of lemon.

Fried herrings

8 fresh herrings, gutted
2 tablespoons lemon juice
½ teaspoon salt
¼ teaspoon pepper
¼ teaspoon paprika pepper
3 tablespoons plain flour
4 tablespoons oil

Rinse the herrings thoroughly, pat dry with kitchen paper and sprinkle inside and out with the lemon juice. Mix together the salt, pepper and paprika and rub inside the herring, then coat the fish with flour. Heat the oil in a pan and fry the fish for 5 minutes on each side. Drain on kitchen paper before serving.

Serve with: Boiled potatoes and pickled beetroot

Top: Quick shrimp sauce; *Left:* Egg and shrimp savoury (page 71); *Right:* Quick shrimp cocktail

Continental poached fish

800 g/1¾ lb filleted white fish
1 clove garlic
2 bunches parsley
2 tablespoons oil
250 ml/8 fl oz chicken stock
salt and pepper to taste
generous pinch dried oregano or marjoram

Wipe the fish fillets, removing the skin and any remaining bones, and pat dry. Peel the garlic and chop finely; wash, dry and chop the parsley. Heat the oil and fry the garlic and parsley, stirring continuously. Gradually add the stock and bring to the boil. Place the fish fillets carefully in the hot liquid, add the seasoning and oregano or marjoram, cover and poach over a low heat for 10 minutes.

Remove the fish and arrange it on a warm dish. Rapidly boil the remaining liquid to reduce it by half, then pour over the fish to serve.

Serve with: Rice or boiled potatoes and green salad or tomato salad

Fish andalouse

800 g/1¾ lb cod or haddock fillet
½ teaspoon salt
juice of 1 lemon
100 g/4 oz cheese, sliced
4 tomatoes
1 onion
2 green peppers
2 heaped tablespoons plain flour
3 tablespoons oil
1 teaspoon paprika pepper

Rinse the fish in cold water, pat dry and cut into equal strips after removing the skin and any bones. Mix the salt into the lemon juice, place the fish strips in this mixture, cover and leave to marinate. Cut the cheese into strips. Slice the tomatoes, peel the onion and cut into rings, then deseed the peppers and cut them into rings.

Coat the fish thoroughly with flour. Heat the oil in a pan and fry the fish until golden brown on both sides, then remove and drain on absorbent kitchen paper. Add the onion and peppers to the pan and fry until soft but not brown. Stir in the tomatoes and cheese, then add the cooked fish and toss lightly until the cheese melts. Serve sprinkled with paprika and chopped parsley, and top with tomato ketchup, if liked.

Savoury fish rolls

4 pieces haddock fillet (each weighing about 150 g/5 oz)
juice of 1 lemon
50 g/2 oz streaky bacon
1 small gherkin
100 g/4 oz Emmental or Edam cheese
1 onion
1 tablespoon mild French mustard
1 tablespoon tomato purée
2 tablespoons oil
100 ml/4 fl oz hot water
150 ml/¼ pint chicken stock
2 teaspoons cornflour
1 (142-ml/5-fl oz) carton soured cream
¼ teaspoon salt
generous pinch of white pepper
1 tablespoon capers

Rinse and skin the fish, dry well and rub with the lemon juice. Cut the bacon, gherkin and cheese into equal strips; peel and finely chop the onion. Spread one side of the fish fillets with half the mustard and all the tomato purée. Divide the bacon, gherkin, cheese and onion between the four fillets, roll them up and secure with wooden cocktail sticks or skewers.

Heat the oil in a pan and fry the fish rolls on all sides. Add the hot water, cover and poach over a low heat for 20 minutes. Heat the stock and towards the end of the cooking time add the hot chicken stock. Take out the fish, place it on a warmed serving dish and keep hot. Mix the cornflour with 1 tablespoon of the soured cream, add a little of the cooking liquid, then stir the mixture into the sauce with the salt, pepper, the rest of the mustard and the capers. Bring slowly to the boil and cook for 1 minute. Pour over the fish rolls and serve.

Serve with: Boiled potatoes or rice and green salad

Fish andalouse

Fish ragoût

675 g / 1½ lb filleted white fish
½ teaspoon salt
juice ½ lemon
100 g / 4 oz Edam or Cheddar cheese
40 g / 1½ oz butter or margarine
3 tablespoons plain flour
450 ml / 15 fl oz milk
pinch each of salt and pepper
pinch of grated nutmeg
2 tablespoons dry sherry
bunch fresh parsley (optional)

Wash and skin the fish fillets, cut into chunks, sprinkle with salt and lemon juice, then cover and leave for 10 minutes. Grate the cheese. Melt the butter or margarine in a pan over low heat, add the flour and cook for 1 minute, stirring all the time. Gradually add the milk and bring to the boil. Put in the fish and cheese, cover and simmer gently for 15 minutes. Season the sauce with the salt, pepper and nutmeg and stir in the dry sherry. Garnish with parsley.

Curried fish and rice

225 g / 8 oz rice
1.15 litres / 2 pints water
2 teaspoons salt
4 fillets cod or haddock (about 150 g / 5 oz each)
juice of ½ lemon
1 onion
1 dessert apple
20 g / ¾ oz butter
2 teaspoons curry powder
2 tablespoons plain flour
500 ml / 16 fl oz chicken stock
generous pinch each of pepper and salt
1 egg yolk
1 tablespoon chopped parsley

Wash the rice, put in the water and add most of the salt. Bring to the boil and simmer for 20 minutes over a low heat. Rinse the fish fillets, pat them dry, sprinkle with the lemon juice and the rest of the salt, cover and leave for several minutes. Peel the onion and cut it into rings. Peel the apple, remove the core and cut into wafer-thin slices.

Melt the butter in a pan and fry the onion, apple and curry powder, stirring continuously. Add the flour and stir for a minute, then gradually pour on the stock. Bring to the boil, put in the fish, cover and simmer gently for 15 minutes. Season the sauce, take off the heat and stir in the egg yolk. Keep the sauce hot but do not allow it to boil again. Strain the rice, turn out on to a plate and arrange it in a ring. Place the curried fish in the middle and garnish with parsley.

Mussel ragoût

65 g / 2½ oz streaky bacon
3 onions
1 leek
500 g / generous 1 lb shelled fresh or bottled or 2 (250-g / 8¾-oz) cans mussels
4 tomatoes
50 g / 2 oz butter
2 tablespoons plain flour
450 ml / ¾ pint milk
½ teaspoon lemon juice
pinch each of salt and pepper
pinch of sugar
bunch fresh or 1 teaspoon dried chopped parsley

Dice the bacon, peel and chop the onions. Halve the leek lengthwise and trim, wash thoroughly and slice. Drain the mussels; wipe and quarter the tomatoes. Melt the butter, add the bacon and onion and cook for 2 minutes, stirring continuously, then add the leek and continue to cook. Stir in the flour, cook for a further minute, then gradually add the milk, stirring constantly. Bring to the boil, add the pieces of tomato and the mussels and season with the lemon juice, salt, pepper and sugar. Simmer over a very gentle heat for 5 minutes without boiling.

Wash, dry and chop the fresh parsley. Garnish the ragoût with this before serving.

Serve with: Rice or pasta

Top: Curried fish and rice; *Bottom:* Fish ragoût

Stuffed fish fillet with caper sauce

675 g / 1½ lb white fish fillet in one piece
½ teaspoon salt
juice ½ lemon
pinch of pepper
pinch of dried thyme
100 g / 4 oz cooked ham
1 gherkin
300 ml / ½ pint boiling water
1 onion
20 g / ¾ oz butter
2 tablespoons plain flour
250 ml / 8 fl oz milk
1 tablespoon capers
100 ml / 4 fl oz white wine

Wash and skin the fish, pat dry and rub with the salt and lemon juice, then season with the pepper and dried thyme. Cut the ham and gherkin into strips and lay them on the fish, roll up the fillet and secure with a skewer or cocktail stick. Place in a shallow pan, cover with the boiling water, cover the pan and cook gently for 15 minutes.

Peel and finely chop the onion. Melt the butter in a pan and fry the onion until soft, stirring constantly. Reducing the heat, stir in the flour and cook for a minute, then gradually add the milk. Bring the sauce slowly to the boil, stirring continuously; add the capers and season with salt and pepper. Remove the fish roll from the cooking liquid, and keep warm. Stir 150 ml / ¼ pint of the cooking liquid into the sauce, add the white wine and heat well without boiling. Place the fish roll on a dish and serve in slices accompanied by the sauce.

Serve with: Green beans, tomatoes and parsley potatoes

Balkan fish casserole

800 g / 1¾ lb white fish fillet
juice of ½ lemon
50 g / 2 oz streaky bacon
3 onions
2 green peppers
1 clove garlic
2 tablespoons oil
2 tablespoons plain flour
2 tablespoons tomato purée
500 ml / 17 fl oz chicken stock
2 teaspoons paprika pepper
pinch of pepper
pinch of dried tarragon

Skin the fish, rinse, dry and sprinkle with the lemon juice. Dice the bacon; peel and finely chop the onions. Cut the peppers into quarters, remove the core and seeds and cut into slices. Peel and finely chop the garlic.
Heat the oil in a pan and fry the bacon, then add the onion, peppers and garlic, stirring constantly. Add the flour and cook for a few minutes over a low heat, still stirring. Add the tomato purée and gradually stir in the stock. Bring to the boil, stirring as it thickens slightly. Cut the fish into small pieces and add to the sauce. Season the sauce with the paprika, pepper and tarragon, cover and simmer over a gentle heat for 12 to 15 minutes.

Serve with: Rice or boiled potatoes and green salad

Left: Stuffed fish fillet with caper sauce. *Right:* Balkan fish casserole

Halibut with tomatoes

4 halibut steaks (each weighing 150 g/5 oz)
$\frac{1}{2}$ teaspoon salt
juice of $\frac{1}{2}$ lemon
2 tablespoons oil
4 tomatoes
20 g/$\frac{3}{4}$ oz butter or margarine
pinch each of salt and pepper
pinch of paprika pepper

Rinse the halibut, sprinkle with salt and lemon juice and leave for about 10 minutes. Heat the oil in a frying pan. Dry the halibut with kitchen paper and fry on both sides over a medium heat for about 15 minutes. Remove from the pan and keep hot. Wipe and dry the tomatoes, cut them into slices and add them with the butter or margarine to the fat in the pan. Fry on both sides over a gentle heat, and season. Arrange the halibut on a dish and cover with the tomato slices to serve.

Serve with: Creamed potato and a green salad

Flemish fish croquettes

500 g/1 lb white fish fillets
2 onions
100 g/4 oz fresh white breadcrumbs
1 egg, beaten
4 tablespoons chopped parsley
pinch of salt
pinch of grated nutmeg
1 teaspoon lemon juice
750 ml/1$\frac{1}{4}$ pints salted water
2 small packets white sauce mix
150 g/5 oz or 1 small can shrimps or prawns
2 tomatoes

Rinse and skin the fish, removing any bones. Dry thoroughly, then cut the fillets into strips and put through the mincer. Peel and finely chop the onions. Mix the minced fish thoroughly with the breadcrumbs, onion, egg and parsley and season with the salt, grated nutmeg and lemon juice. Bring the salted water to the boil, dampen your hands and form 8 croquettes from the fish mixture. Lower them carefully into the boiling water and simmer for 10 minutes. Make up the sauce according to the directions on the packets. Drain

the fish croquettes and add to the sauce, together with the drained shrimps or prawns. Slit the tomatoes at one end, cover with boiling water and leave for a minute. Peel off the skins, cut the flesh into pieces, discarding the seeds, and add to the sauce. Continue to cook for a few more minutes.

Haddock provençale

1 small haddock (weighing about 1.25 g/2$\frac{3}{4}$ lb)
juice of 1 lemon
1 bay leaf
3 peppercorns
$\frac{1}{2}$ teaspoon salt
3 onions
3 cloves garlic
3 tablespoons oil
2 tablespoons flour
1 tablespoon tomato purée
pinch each of salt and pepper
100 ml/4 fl oz white wine
small sprig of parsley and twists of lemon to garnish

Rinse the fish thoroughly, dry and sprinkle inside and out with the lemon juice. Put 1.5 litres/2$\frac{3}{4}$ pints water into a fish kettle, add the bay leaf, peppercorns and salt and bring the water to the boil. Peel one of the onions and cut it into eight pieces; peel and quarter one clove of garlic. Add both to the boiling water and put in the fish. Reduce the heat and simmer for 20 minutes. Peel and chop the remaining onions; peel the other garlic cloves and chop finely.

Heat the oil in a pan and fry the onion and garlic, stirring constantly. Reducing the heat, add the flour and cook for 2 minutes, stirring continuously. Add the tomato purée and gradually stir in 250 ml/8 fl oz of the cooking liquid and bring to the boil. Season the sauce with salt and pepper and add the white wine. Stir well, but do not allow to boil again. Arrange the cooked fish on a warm dish, pour over the sauce and garnish with the parsley and lemon twists.

Serve with: Parsley potatoes

Top: Halibut with tomatoes; variation of Country-style chicken soup (page 8); *Bottom:* Haddock provençale

Seafood kebabs

400 g/14 oz prawns, canned or frozen
400 g/14 oz fillet of sole or plaice
½ cucumber
1 onion
8 stuffed olives
1 tablespoon oil
100 ml/4 fl oz tomato ketchup
4 tablespoons water
2 tablespoons single cream
2 teaspoons paprika pepper

Cover the prawns and sole and if frozen allow to thaw at room temperature for 3 to 4 hours. Wipe the cucumber and, without peeling, cut it into thick slices. Peel the onion and cut into eight pieces. Cut the sole into strips and thread these alternately with slices of cucumber, onion pieces and olives on four skewers. Heat the oil in a pan and fry the kebabs over medium heat for 8 to 10 minutes, turning frequently. Remove and keep hot. Mix the tomato ketchup with the prawns, water, cream and paprika. Add to the juices in the pan and heat through, stirring continuously, to make a sauce to serve with the kebabs.

Seafood ragoût

500 g/1 lb cod or haddock fillet, fresh or frozen
1 onion
1 green pepper
250 g/8 oz mushrooms
350 g/12 oz prawns, canned or frozen
3 tablespoons soy sauce
2 tablespoons oil
½ cup white wine
½ teaspoon celery salt

Rinse the fish fillets, if fresh. Allow to thaw, if frozen, until they can be separated. Peel the onion and cut into eight pieces. Halve the pepper, remove the seeds, and wash and chop the flesh. Wipe or peel the mushrooms. Drain and separate the prawns, if canned, then cut the fish fillet into equal pieces with a serrated knife. Mix the soy sauce with the oil, white wine and celery salt, pour over all the ingredients, cover and leave to marinate in the refrigerator for 4 hours.
Place the fish, onions, prawns, mushrooms and pepper in a pan with the liquid from the marinade

and 250 ml/8 fl oz hot water. Cover and cook over a gentle heat for 30 minutes.

Bohemian herrings

8 rollmop herrings or kipper fillets
2 onions
1 lemon
10 small gherkins
a few sprigs parsley
2 sticks celery
2 carrots
350 ml/12 fl oz water
100 ml/4 fl oz vinegar
2 bay leaves
3 peppercorns
2 teaspoons small capers
250 ml/8 fl oz soured cream

Soak the herrings or kipper fillets for 12 hours, changing the water repeatedly. Peel the onions and cut into rings; pare off the lemon rind as thinly as possible. Cut the gherkins into strips; wash and chop the parsley. Wash the celery thoroughly and chop; clean the carrots, scrape and slice thinly. Boil the water with the vinegar, bay leaves, peppercorns, onion rings, carrot, parsley and celery for 20 minutes. Put the fillets in a dish, cover with the lemon peel, capers and half the gherkins and pour on the vinegar marinade, including the herbs and vegetables. Cover and leave to marinate overnight. Drain, pour on the soured cream and garnish with the rest of the gherkins.

Bohemian herrings

Braised beef in cider

(Illustrated on page 26)

FOR THE BEEF
1 clove garlic
2 onions
2 green peppers
1 kg/2 lb brisket of beef
½ teaspoon salt
pinch each of pepper, cayenne pepper and
paprika pepper
1 teaspoon chopped dried oregano or marjoram
2 tablespoons oil
475 ml/16 fl oz beef stock
1 tablespoon plain flour
25 g/1 oz butter
FOR THE CABBAGE
1 kg/2 lb white cabbage
150 ml/5 fl oz dry cider
½ teaspoon salt
¼ teaspoon white pepper
1 teaspoon caraway
1 teaspoon sugar
dash of vinegar

Peel and chop the garlic finely; peel and chop the onions. Halve the peppers, remove the seeds and cut into thin slices. Buy the meat boned in a flat piece: wipe, dry well and rub it with the salt, pepper, cayenne, paprika and oregano or marjoram. Scatter the garlic, onion and peppers over the meat, roll it up and tie it firmly with string. Preheat the oven to moderate (180 C, 350 F, Gas Mark 4). Heat the oil in a large frying pan and briskly fry the meat on all sides to seal in the juices. Place the joint in a roasting tin with the stock and braise for 90 minutes, basting several times during cooking. After 90 minutes, turn off the oven and leave in the meat for 10 minutes to keep warm. Beat the flour into the butter until smooth. Pour the juices from the meat into a saucepan, heat gently and add the butter and flour mixture in small pieces, whisking continuously until it melts and the sauce boils and thickens.

While the meat is cooking, remove the outer leaves of the cabbage, cut it into quarters, trim out the stem and shred the leaves. Cook in boiling salted water until just tender; drain thoroughly. Heat the cider, add the drained cabbage, salt, pepper, caraway, sugar and vinegar, stir well, cover and simmer slowly for 15 minutes.

Cut the joint into slices, place the cabbage on a dish and arrange the meat slices on top. Serve the sauce separately. If required for freezing, before carving set aside half the meat and half the quantity of cabbage to cool.

Suitable for freezing

Beef and cauliflower hotpot

(Illustrated on page 26)

450 g/1 lb stewing beef, cubed
mixed casserole vegetables in season (onion,
celery, leek)
3 carrots
25 g/1 oz butter
1.5 litres/2¾ pints beef stock
salt to taste
100 g/4 oz rice
1 cauliflower
generous pinch of pepper
generous pinch of ground coriander
1 bunch parsley

Wipe the meat; wash, prepare and chop the mixed vegetables. Clean, peel and slice the carrots. Melt the butter in a heavy-based pan, add the beef and cook, turning constantly, for a few minutes until browned. Add the stock and the vegetables, season to taste and bring to the boil. Cover and simmer gently for approximately 2 hours.

Wash the rice, if necessary, and drain. Trim and wash the cauliflower, divide into florets and cut away the thick stem. Add the rice and cauliflower to the hotpot, cover and simmer over a gentle heat for 25 to 30 minutes. Season with the pepper and ground coriander. Wash, drain and chop the parsley and add to the hotpot before serving.

Layered beef hotpot

500 g/1 lb braising steak
2 tablespoons oil
8 small potatoes
2 onions
3 leeks
2 carrots
6 stalks celery
salt and pepper
600 ml/1 pint beef stock
4 tablespoons chopped parsley

Wipe the beef, remove sinews, membrane and fat and cut into equal pieces. Heat the oil in a frying pan, add the meat and brown on all sides, then transfer it to a plate. Peel and dice the potatoes, peel and chop the onions. Remove the ends and any damaged outer leaves from the leeks, cut in half lengthwise, wash thoroughly in cold water and slice. Scrape or peel the carrots and slice, wash and chop the celery.

Place the meat and prepared vegetables in alternate layers in a heavy-based flameproof casserole, seasoning each layer with salt and pepper. Pour over the stock, cover and simmer very gently for 2 hours. Sprinkle with parsley.

Bavarian goulash

400 g/14 oz chuck or stewing steak
3 onions
2 cloves garlic
4 peppers
20 g/$\frac{3}{4}$ oz lard or oil
1 teaspoon salt
1 teaspoon paprika pepper
1 teaspoon caraway seeds
150 ml/5 fl oz beer
100 ml/4 fl oz water
500 g/1 lb sauerkraut
100 ml/4 fl oz soured cream

Trim the meat and cut into equal pieces. Peel the onions and the garlic and chop finely. Halve the

peppers, remove the seeds and cores and cut into eight pieces, reserving a few for garnish. Heat the lard or oil in a pan and brown the meat quickly on all sides. Add the onion, garlic, salt and peppers to the meat and fry for 5 minutes, stirring constantly. Add the paprika, caraway, beer and water, then cover and cook for several minutes. Separate the sauerkraut with two spoons and mix with the meat. Cover and cook gently over a low heat for 50 minutes. Before serving, stir in the soured cream and season well once more. Garnish with the fresh pepper pieces.

Hungarian mince

4 peppers
3 onions
3 tomatoes
2 tablespoons oil
350 g/12 oz minced beef
300 ml/$\frac{1}{2}$ pint beef stock
pinch each of salt and pepper
1 tablespoon paprika pepper

Halve the peppers, remove the cores and seeds and slice. Peel and chop the onions. Slit the tomatoes at one end, cover with boiling water and leave for a minute, then peel and cut into pieces. Heat the oil in a pan and fry the onions until transparent, stirring constantly. Add the peppers and fry, then add the minced beef and continue frying, stirring all the time to ensure even browning. Stir in the stock and tomato, season with salt, pepper and paprika, cover and cook over a gentle heat for 20 minutes.

Left, clockwise from the top: Hungarian mince; Beef and cauliflower hotpot (page 25); Braised beef in cider (page 25); Savoury beef pancakes (page 68). *Right:* Bavarian goulash

Calves' tongue with mushroom sauce

800 g/1¾ lb calves' tongue
mixed casserole vegetables as available (carrots,
celery, leek)
1 onion
2 litres/3½ pints water
4 peppercorns
1 bay leaf
2 cloves
1 teaspoon salt
25 g/1 oz butter
1 tablespoon flour
200 g/6 oz mushrooms
1 teaspoon lemon juice
2 egg yolks
5 tablespoons single cream
pinch of sugar
pinch of white pepper
4 tablespoons chopped parsley

Buy the calves' tongue and have any sinews, fat and gristle already removed. Rinse tongue in cold water. Wash and chop the mixed vegetables finely, peel and quarter the onion. Bring the water to the boil, add all the vegetables, the peppercorns, bay leaf, cloves, salt and tongue and simmer for 1½ hours over a low heat. The tongue is cooked when the tip is tender.

Drain the meat, cut away the outer white skin and remove any remaining gristle. Cut the tongue into slices about 2.5 cm/1 inch thick and keep hot. Strain 500 ml/17 fl oz of the cooking liquid and put aside. Melt the butter in a small pan, add the flour and cook for a minute, stirring continuously. Gradually add the reserved cooking liquid and bring to the boil. Slice the mushrooms and add to the sauce with the lemon juice; heat gently for a few minutes.

Beat the egg yolks with the cream, sugar and pepper, and stir in a little of the hot sauce. Remove the sauce from the heat and stir in the egg and cream mixture. Garnish with the parsley and serve with the tongue.

Serve with: Boiled potatoes and green peas tossed in butter

Beef roulades

4 slices topside (each about 100 g/4 oz)
pinch each of salt and pepper
1 teaspoon mild French mustard
1 gherkin
2 onions
100 g/4 oz streaky bacon, derinded
3 tablespoons oil
1 tablespoon flour
450 ml/¾ pint beef stock

Place the meat slices between greaseproof paper and beat until thin. Season with the salt and pepper and spread with the mustard. Cut the gherkin lengthwise into quarters. Peel the onions, chopping one and quartering the other. Divide the gherkin, chopped onion and half the bacon between the beef slices. Roll up and tie securely with string. Dice the rest of the bacon.

Heat the oil in a pan and brown the meat rolls quickly on all sides. Add the onion quarters and bacon and cook for a few minutes. Add the flour, stir well, then gradually add the stock, stirring continuously. Cover and simmer for 1 hour.

Boiled beef

1.5 litres/2¾ pints water
1 teaspoon salt
1 onion
1 kg/2¼ lb brisket or silverside
1 bay leaf
1 clove
4 peppercorns
mixed casserole vegetables as available (carrot,
celery, leek)

Bring the water and salt to the boil. Peel the onion and cut into eight. Put the meat into the water with the bay leaf, onion, clove and peppercorns, cover and simmer over a low heat for 2½ hours, adding a little extra water if necessary. Wash and chop the mixed vegetables and add to the liquid after 2 hours' cooking time. Remove the cooked meat about half an hour later, strain the stock and keep to use for a soup. Serve the meat surrounded by the cooked vegetables.

Fillet of beef with crusted almonds

Fillet of beef with crusted almonds

500 g / 1 lb fillet of beef
1 tablespoon oil
½ teaspoon salt
pinch of pepper
pinch of paprika pepper
pinch of ground ginger
40 g / 1½ oz butter or margarine
2 egg yolks
50 g / 2 oz flaked almonds

Preheat the oven to hot (230 C, 450 F, Gas Mark 8). Mix the oil with the salt, pepper, paprika and ginger and coat the meat on all sides, then put it in the centre of the oven and roast for 30 to 40 minutes. Beat the butter with the egg yolks, gradually working them in, and finally mix the almonds into the foamy mass. Coat the top of the meat with the almond mixture and cook for a further 10 minutes so that a crust is formed. Serve immediately.

Serve with: Young carrots and green beans tossed in butter

Braised steak

Braised steak

4 slices shin of beef or braising steak (each
about 250 g/9 oz)
1 large onion
2 tablespoons oil
1 clove garlic, crushed
½ teaspoon salt
generous pinch of pepper
100 ml/4 fl oz red wine
375 ml/13 fl oz beef stock
2 large carrots
1 small head celery
1 pepper
1 bunch parsley
150 ml/5 fl oz soured cream (optional)

Wipe and trim the meat. Peel and roughly chop the onion. Heat the oil and fry the onion and garlic well, stirring constantly. Add the meat, brown quickly on all sides, season with salt and pepper, then add the wine and stock; cover and simmer for 1¾ hours. Peel and dice the carrots and wash and chop the celery. Halve the pepper, remove the seeds and slice. Thirty minutes before the end of the cooking time, add the vegetables to the meat and continue to simmer. Wash, drain and chop the parsley. Stir the cream, if used, into the stock and vegetables, adjust the seasoning and serve immediately, garnished with the parsley.

Serve with: Rice or pasta

Rich beef stew

675 g/1½ lb brisket of beef
50 g/2 oz streaky bacon, derinded
mixed casserole vegetables as available (carrot,
celery, leek)
2 onions
½ teaspoon salt
¼ teaspoon pepper
1 teaspoon mild French mustard
2 tablespoons oil
1 bay leaf
300 ml/½ pint red wine
900 ml/1½ pints beef stock
1 tablespoon cornflour
5 tablespoons single cream

Wipe the meat and dice the bacon. Wash and chop
the casserole vegetables; peel and chop the
onions. Rub the meat thoroughly with the salt,
pepper and mustard. Heat the oil in a pan and
brown the meat quickly on all sides over a high
heat. Add the bacon, mixed vegetables, onion and
bay leaf and cook for a few minutes. Pour in the
red wine and stock, cover and simmer over a low
heat for 2 hours. Remove the meat and keep hot.
Take out the bay leaf and reduce the stock by
boiling for 15 minutes, uncovered. Mix the
cornflour with a little cold water and add it to the
stock; return to the heat, bring to the boil and
cook for a few minutes to thicken. Finally stir in
the cream. Slice the meat, pour over a little sauce
and serve the rest separately.

Beef and onion casserole

1 onion
4 slices topside (each about 100 g/4 oz)
2 teaspoons mild French mustard
¼ teaspoon salt
¼ teaspoon pepper
2 tablespoons oil
1 tablespoon flour
500 ml/17 fl oz meat stock

Peel the onion and cut into rings. Spread the meat
with the mustard and season with the salt and
pepper. Heat the oil in a pan, fry the meat quickly
on both sides over a high heat and then remove.
Fry the onion rings and take them out when
lightly browned. Add the flour to the oil and cook
over a reduced heat, stirring continuously.
Gradually pour on the stock and bring to the boil.
Return the meat and onions to the pan, cover and
simmer gently for 50 minutes over a low heat.

Steak kebabs

500 g/1 lb rump steak
2 apples
2 green peppers
2 red peppers
1 large onion
2 tablespoons oil
1 teaspoon salt
generous pinch of pepper
generous pinch of paprika pepper

Wipe the meat and cut into equal pieces. Wash
and dry the apples and without peeling, cut into
slices about 2 cm/1 inch thick. Halve the peppers,
remove the seeds and dice coarsely. Peel and cut
the onion into large pieces. Place the pieces of
meat, apple, peppers and onion alternately on a
large skewer. Mix the oil with the salt, pepper
and paprika and brush on so that the skewered
pieces are well coated. Cook for 20 minutes on a
rotating spit or under the grill. If you do not have
a spit the skewer must be turned several times
during cooking.

Kidney kebabs

250 g/8 oz calves' kidney
500 g/1 lb fillet of veal
2 onions
1 (75-g/2¾-oz) can red peppers (pimientos)
20 g/¾ oz butter
¼ teaspoon each of salt, pepper and paprika
pepper

Preheat the grill to the hottest setting. Cut the calves' kidneys in half lengthwise, remove all veins, sinews, fat and the core and soak for a short time in water. Wipe the veal and cut into equal pieces. Peel the onions and cut into rings, then drain the peppers and cut into equal pieces. Remove the kidney from the water, pat dry and cut into cubes.

Melt the butter and stir in the salt, pepper and paprika. Place the pieces of kidney, veal and red pepper alternately on four skewers and lay the onion rings on top. Baste the kebabs thoroughly with the seasoned butter, then grill for 15 minutes, turning frequently to ensure that they are cooked on all sides.

Serve with: Curried rice

Veal goulash Piroschka

575 g/1¼ lb stewing veal
2 onions
40 g/1½ oz butter or margarine
500 ml/17 fl oz beef stock
½ teaspoon salt
1 pepper
4 tomatoes
½ clove garlic
150 ml/¼ pint soured cream
2 tablespoons tomato purée
1 tablespoon paprika pepper

Remove any sinews and membrane from the veal and cut into equal bite-sized pieces. Peel and chop the onions. Heat the butter or margarine in a pan, brown the meat on all sides, add the onion and fry for 5 minutes, stirring continuously. Pour the stock over the meat, add the salt, then cover and simmer over a low heat for about an hour. Halve, deseed and slice the pepper. Cut through the tomatoes at one end, cover with boiling water and leave for a minute, then peel and roughly chop. After an hour's cooking time, add the pepper and tomato to the meat, then cover and cook for a further 15 minutes over a very low heat. Peel and chop the garlic and crush with the blade of a knife. Mix the soured cream with the garlic, tomato purée and paprika and stir into the goulash. Serve immediately.

Serve with: Rice or boiled potatoes and green salad

Braised veal

675 g/1½ lb loin of veal or pork
¼ teaspoon salt
¼ teaspoon pepper
1 tablespoon oil
mixed casserole vegetables as available (onion,
carrot, celery, leek)
250 ml/8 fl oz meat or chicken stock
25 g/1 oz butter
1 tablespoon flour
1 (100-g/4-oz) carton single cream

Buy the veal or pork already boned and rolled. Preheat the oven to moderately hot (200 C, 400 F, Gas Mark 6). Mix well together the salt, pepper and oil, then place the joint in the roasting tin and brush with the seasoned oil. Wash and finely chop the mixed vegetables, and arrange in the roasting tin with the meat. Pour over the stock and cook, covered, for 50 minutes. Transfer the meat and vegetables to a warmed serving dish and keep hot. Blend the butter with the flour until smooth and add in small pieces to the juices in the roasting tin, stirring over a low heat until the liquid thickens and boils. Stir in the cream, adjust the seasoning and heat gently. Serve the meat accompanied by the sauce.

Serve with: Buttered carrots and mashed potato

Opposite page, left: Kidney kebabs; *Back right:* Hot veal pie (page 34); *Bottom right:* Braised veal

Hot veal pie

(Illustrated on page 33)

FOR THE PASTRY:
225 g/8 oz plain flour
pinch of salt
100 g/4 oz butter or margarine
1 egg, lightly beaten
1 egg yolk
FOR THE FILLING:
800 g/1¾ lb stewing veal
1 tablespoon plain flour
2 onions
1 carrot
2 tablespoons oil
¼ teaspoon salt
pinch of pepper
300 ml/½ pint chicken stock

For the pastry, sieve the flour and salt into a bowl. Cut the butter or margarine into small pieces and rub into the flour until the mixture resembles fine breadcrumbs. Bind together with the lightly beaten egg to make a smooth dough, then leave for at least 30 minutes in the refrigerator.

Wipe and trim the meat, cut into equal dice and toss in the flour. Peel the onions and cut into rings; wash, scrape and dice the carrot. Heat the oil in a pan and brown the veal pieces on all sides. Add the onion rings and carrot, season with salt and pepper and fry for 5 minutes, stirring continuously. Pour on the stock, cover and simmer over a low heat for 30 minutes.

Grease an ovenproof dish or 1.15-litre/2-pint pie dish and preheat the oven to moderately hot (200 C, 400 F, Gas Mark 6). Remove the cooked meat from the heat and allow to cool. Roll out the pastry approximately 1 cm/½ inch thick and use two-thirds to line the dish. Fill with the cooked meat mixture and cover with the rest of the pastry. Beat the egg yolk, prick the pastry top with a fork and brush with the egg yolk. Bake the pie for 45 to 50 minutes until golden brown.

Quick veal cutlets

(Illustrated below)

4 veal cutlets (each about 150 g/5 oz)
2 tablespoons oil
pinch of salt and pepper for each cutlet
4 tablespoons canned crushed pineapple
4 tablespoons shredded carrot or white cabbage

Wipe the cutlets. Heat the oil in a pan and fry the cutlets for 1 minute on each side over a high heat, then turn down the heat to medium and fry for a further 4 minutes on each side. After frying, season with salt and pepper, place on a dish and keep hot. Mix the crushed pineapple with the coleslaw and use to garnish the cutlets for serving.

Serve with: French bread or parsley potatoes

Ragoût of veal

500 g/1 lb stewing veal
50 g/2 oz streaky bacon, derinded
40 g/1½ oz butter or margarine
1 tablespoon flour
1 tablespoon paprika pepper
pinch of cayenne pepper
pinch of white pepper
250 ml/8 fl oz chicken stock
4 tablespoons single cream
4 tablespoons chopped parsley

Wipe the meat, remove any membranes and sinews and cut into thick pieces. Dice the bacon. Melt the butter or margarine in a pan and fry the meat and bacon for 5 minutes, stirring constantly. Sprinkle on the flour, add the paprika, cayenne and white pepper and fry over a medium heat for a further 2 minutes. Add the stock and bring it to the boil, then cover and simmer over a low heat for 45 minutes. Remove from the heat, stir in the cream and garnish with parsley before serving.

Serve with: Dumplings or pasta and green salad

Veal and vegetable hotpot

(Illustrated on page 36)

1 small head of cauliflower
dash of vinegar
500 g/1 lb stewing steak or pie veal
2 onions
3 tablespoons oil
750 ml/1¼ pints beef stock
generous pinch of salt
500 g/1 lb potatoes
300 g/12 oz carrots
300 g/12 oz French beans
pinch of pepper

Place the cauliflower, florets downwards, in water with a dash of added vinegar. Remove membrane, sinews and fat from the meat and cut into bite-sized pieces. Peel the onions and cut into rings.

Heat the oil in a heavy-based flameproof casserole or saucepan and fry the onion rings and meat for 5 minutes until brown. Add the stock and salt, cover and simmer over a low heat for 1½ hours. Peel and dice the potatoes; wash, scrape or peel and slice the carrots. Wash and trim the beans, cutting up any large ones. Take the cauliflower out of the water and cut into florets, removing any thick stalk. Add the cauliflower and carrots to the meat and cook for 10 minutes, then add the potatoes and beans. Cover and cook for a further 30 minutes. Season to taste before serving.

Spicy lamb stew

500 g/1 lb boneless lean lamb (off the leg)
2 onions
2 tablespoons oil
3 tablespoons tomato purée
1 teaspoon caraway seeds
1 tablespoon paprika pepper
450 ml/¾ pint chicken stock
4 tablespoons chopped parsley

Wipe the meat and cut into equal pieces; peel and finely chop the onions. Heat the oil in a pan, fry the onion briskly and, stirring constantly, add the meat and brown quickly on all sides. Add the tomato purée, caraway and paprika and gradually stir in the stock, then cover and stew over a gentle heat for 1½ hours. Sprinkle with parsley before serving.

Below: Veal and vegetable hotpot (page 35).
Right: Festive lamb

Festive lamb

1–2 cloves garlic
1 carrot
2 onions
1 kg/2¼ lb boned leg of lamb
1 teaspoon salt
¼ teaspoon pepper
2 tablespoons oil
300 ml/½ pint chicken stock
100 ml/4 fl oz red wine
1 tablespoon plain flour
25 g/1 oz butter
100 ml/4 fl oz soured cream

Peel and chop the garlic finely. Scrape, wash and dice the carrot. Peel the onions and cut each into eight pieces. Remove any sinews and membrane from the meat, wipe clean and rub the surface with the salt and pepper. Preheat the oven to moderately hot (200 C, 400 F, Gas Mark 6). Heat the oil in the roasting tin, then put in the meat and arrange the garlic, carrot and onion around the joint. Cook in the oven for 1½ hours. After 30 minutes add the stock and wine and cover the meat. Take off the cover again for the last 15 minutes of the cooking time. Transfer the joint to a warmed serving dish and keep hot. Blend the flour with the butter until smooth and, stirring continuously, add it in small pieces to the juices in the roasting tin. Bring the juices to the boil to thicken. Season, then stir the soured cream into the sauce and serve separately.

If the meat is divided into two pieces, one half can be sliced and served with the sauce and the other half can be frozen or kept aside for another meal, such as a hotpot.

Serve with: Green beans tossed in butter, steamed tomatoes and potato croquettes

Suitable for freezing

Lamb casserole

450 g / 1 lb middle or scrag end of neck of lamb
200 g / 7 oz streaky bacon, derinded
500 ml / 17 fl oz chicken stock
12 small potatoes
500 g / 1 lb white cabbage
500 g / 1 lb baby carrots, fresh or canned
salt and pepper

Wipe the meat and remove excess fat. Cut the bacon into small pieces, put into a heavy-based flameproof casserole or saucepan and cook very slowly, stirring continuously. Add the lamb and brown on all sides, stirring constantly. Heat the stock and pour it over the meat, then cover and simmer over a medium heat. Wash, peel and halve the potatoes and add to the meat. Continue to cook over a low heat for 2 hours. Removing the stalks and outside leaves, wash the cabbage and cut into small pieces. Fifteen minutes before the end of the cooking time add the cabbage and the carrots with a little of the liquid from the can, if canned are used. Season to taste and cook for the remaining time.

Stuffed cabbage rolls in tomato sauce

8 large cabbage leaves, washed and trimmed
1 onion
50 g / 2 oz fresh white breadcrumbs
1 egg, lightly beaten
pinch each of salt and pepper
1 teaspoon paprika pepper
500 g / 1 lb minced pork or beef
600 ml / 1 pint chicken stock
2 tablespoons concentrated tomato purée
2 teaspoons cornflour

Blanch the cabbage in boiling water for 3 minutes and drain. Peel and finely chop the onion. Mix the breadcrumbs with the onion, egg, salt, pepper, paprika and mince. Divide the mixture into 8 portions and place each on a cabbage leaf, then fold the sides over the filling and roll up the leaves to form neat parcels, securing them with string.

Put the cabbage rolls in a pan, add the stock and tomato purée, cover and simmer for 1½ hours. When cooked, transfer the rolls to a warmed serving dish. Mix the cornflour with a little cold water and stir into the tomato sauce; bring to the boil, stirring continuously, and cook for 2 minutes. Adjust the seasoning, pour over the cabbage and serve immediately.

Meatballs in horseradish sauce

1 onion
250 g / 9 oz minced beef
150 g / 5 oz minced pork
50 g / 2 oz fresh white breadcrumbs
50 g / 2 oz butter or margarine
1 egg
¼ teaspoon salt
generous pinch of pepper
generous pinch grated nutmeg
2 tablespoons dried breadcrumbs
2 tablespoons flour
150 ml / 5 fl oz meat stock
250 ml / 8 fl oz milk
200 g / 7 oz grated horseradish
½ teaspoon sugar
175 ml / 6 fl oz single cream

Peel and finely chop the onion, then mix it with the beef and pork mince and breadcrumbs. Melt half the butter or margarine and use to bind the meat mixture together with the egg, salt, pepper and nutmeg. Wet your hands and shape the mixture into meatballs about the size of plums, then coat each carefully with dried breadcrumbs. Melt the remaining butter or margarine in a pan, add the meatballs and fry until brown, turning them frequently so that they brown evenly. Take out the meatballs and sprinkle in the flour, cook for a few minutes, stirring continuously, then gradually mix in the stock and milk and bring to the boil. Add the horseradish and sugar to the sauce, stir well, then put in the meatballs and simmer over a low heat for 20 minutes. Remove from the heat and stir in the cream.

Serve with: Mashed potato and green salad

Lamb casserole

Stuffed meat loaf

3 eggs
3 onions
100 g/4 oz fresh white breadcrumbs
675 g/1½ lb minced lamb or beef
1 teaspoon mild French mustard
½ teaspoon salt
¼ teaspoon pepper
1 tablespoon oil

Hard boil two of the eggs, peel and chop the onions. Add the breadcrumbs to the minced meat and add the onion. Break and add the other egg to bind the mixture. Add the mustard, salt and pepper and work the ingredients into a malleable mixture. Preheat the oven to moderate (180 C, 350 F, Gas Mark 4). Grease a loaf tin with a little oil and fill with half the meat mixture. Cool and peel the two hard-boiled eggs, place lengthwise on the meat and cover with the rest of the meat mixture. Brush with the rest of the oil and bake in the oven for about 1 hour. Turn out on a warmed dish for serving.

Serve with: Peas, carrots or green beans tossed in butter, and mashed potato

Mock cutlets

1 onion
400 g/14 oz minced lamb or beef
25 g/1 oz fresh white breadcrumbs
1 egg, lightly beaten
½ teaspoon mild French mustard
½ teaspoon salt
pinch of pepper
pinch of paprika pepper
4 tablespoons dried breadcrumbs
2 tablespoons oil

Peel and chop the onion. Mix together the meat, fresh breadcrumbs and onion, then bind with the egg. Add the mustard, salt, pepper and paprika and shape into four flat cutlets, wetting your hands to stop the mixture sticking. Coat each cutlet carefully with breadcrumbs, heat the oil and fry the cutlets slowly for 5 minutes on each side.

Serve with: Braised vegetables in white sauce such as celery, cauliflower or mushrooms, creamed potatoes or a crisp salad

Liver sauté

(Illustrated on page 42)

4 slices liver (each about 150 g/5 oz)
1 onion
3 tablespoons oil
generous pinch of salt and pepper
4 slices freshly made toast
4 sprigs parsley

Wash the liver quickly, dry and trim. Peel the onion and cut into rings. Heat the oil in a pan and fry the liver gently on each side for 3 minutes. Season the liver with salt and pepper and place a slice on each piece of toast. Fry the onion rings in the remaining fat, divide between the liver slices and garnish each slice with a sprig of parsley.

Serve with: Chicory and orange salad

Top: Stuffed meat loaf; *Bottom:* Mock cutlets

Left: Liver sauté (page 41); Chicory and orange salad (page 57).
Below: Braised leg of pork

Braised leg of pork

1 kg/2¼ lb leg of pork
2 tablespoons oil
50 g/2 oz streaky bacon
250 ml/8 fl oz hot meat stock
200 g/7 oz mushrooms
3 tomatoes
generous pinch each of salt and pepper
generous pinch cayenne pepper
4 tablespoons single cream

Wipe the meat and preheat the oven to moderately hot (200 C, 400 F, Gas Mark 6). Heat the oil in a roasting tin, put in the meat, lay the bacon slices over it and cook for 15 minutes. Pour the stock around the meat and continue to cook for a further 50 to 60 minutes, basting frequently. Wash or peel the mushrooms and slice thinly. Cut the tomatoes at one end, cover with boiling water and leave for a minute, then peel and cut into pieces, discarding the seeds. Add the tomatoes, mushrooms, salt, pepper and cayenne to the stock for the last 10 minutes of the cooking time. Take out the roasting tin and transfer the meat to a warmed serving dish. Stir the cream into the pan juices, adjust the seasoning and serve separately.

Serve with: Dumplings or pasta

Pork with olives in caraway sauce

1 to 2 teaspoons caraway seeds
10 stoneless green olives
1 tablespoon oil
575 g/1¼ lb pork tenderloin
½ teaspoon salt
1 teaspoon paprika pepper
1 tablespoon tomato purée
150 ml/¼ pint chicken stock
2 tablespoons brandy
4 tablespoons single cream

Crush the caraway finely. Rinse the olives quickly in cold water, drain and slice. Heat the oil in a pan and fry the pork on all sides for a total of 4 minutes. Take out the meat, cut across the grain into diagonal slices and sprinkle with the salt and paprika. Mix together the tomato purée, stock, brandy and add caraway to taste. Stirring continuously, bring the sauce to the boil, add the seasoned pork and the sliced olives, then cover and simmer over a low heat for 20 minutes. Stir in the cream and heat gently for a few minutes before serving.

Pork and beef kebabs

350 g/12 oz lean boneless pork
250 g/8 oz rump steak
3 tomatoes
2 pickled cucumbers
1 onion
3 tablespoons oil
generous pinch of salt for each kebab
generous pinch of cayenne pepper for each kebab

Trim the meat and cut into equal pieces. Quarter the tomatoes and cut the pickled cucumbers into 2-cm/1-inch thick slices. Peel the onion and cut into eight. Place the meat, tomatoes, cucumbers and onion alternately on four skewers. Heat the oil in a pan and fry the kebabs for a total of 12 minutes over a low heat, turning constantly. Before serving, season the kebabs with salt and cayenne pepper to taste.

Serve with: Curried rice and a mixed salad

Savoury mince puff

1 (368-g/12-oz packet frozen puff pastry
1 onion
1 small green pepper
25 g/1 oz butter
½ teaspoon paprika pepper
generous pinch of salt and pepper
225 g/8 oz minced pork
225 g/8 oz minced beef
25 g/1 oz fresh white breadcrumbs
1 egg, lightly beaten
2 tablespoons chopped parsley

Roll the pastry out to an oblong measuring 20 × 25 cm/8 × 10 inches. Peel the onion, halve and deseed the green pepper and finely chop them. Melt the butter in a frying pan, add the onion, pepper, paprika and seasoning and cook the vegetables until soft but not browned. Remove from the heat and mix with the minced meat. Stir in the breadcrumbs and most of the beaten egg, reserving a little to glaze the pastry. Finally mix in the chopped parsley and stir well to ensure that the ingredients are thoroughly combined.

Arrange the meat mixture down the middle of the pastry oblong and dampen the pastry edges, folding them up over the top of the meat and pressing them together to seal them. Seal the ends and use any pastry cuttings to decorate the top. Brush lightly with the reserved egg and carefully lift on to a lightly greased baking tray. Bake in a hot oven (220 C, 425 F, Gas Mark 7) for 15 minutes, then reduce the oven temperature to moderate (180 C, 350 F, Gas Mark 4) and cook for a further 30 minutes.

Serve with: Creamed potatoes and a green salad

Pork and beef kebabs

Poultry and game

Chicken curry with chilled vegetable moulds

FOR THE VEGETABLES
20 g/¾ oz powdered gelatine
600 ml/1 pint chicken stock, cooled
1 egg
450 g/1 lb cooked vegetables (carrot, onion,
pepper, cauliflower florets)
5 red stuffed green olives
3 gherkins
FOR THE CHICKEN CURRY
1 small roasting chicken
1 tablespoon flour
pinch each of salt and pepper
pinch of ground ginger
1 tablespoon curry powder
1 carrot
1 onion
½ leek
¼ head of celery
1 tablespoon oil
500 ml/17 fl oz hot chicken stock
½ teaspoon grated lemon peel
1 tablespoon flaked coconut

Pour 2 tablespoons hot water into a bowl and
stand it in a pan of boiling water. Sprinkle with
gelatine and stir until dissolved, then take off the
heat and add the stock. Hard boil the egg. Dice
the mixed vegetables, rinse the olives and gherkins in cold water, drain and slice; cool, peel and
slice the egg. Pour a little gelatine mixture into
four individual moulds and add 1 egg slice. Pour
over a little more gelatine. Divide the mixed
vegetables, gherkins and olives between the
moulds and cover with the remaining gelatine
mixture. Leave in the refrigerator to set.
Clean and joint the chicken and dust with the
flour, seasoning, ginger and curry powder. Wash,
scrape and cut the carrot into pieces; peel and
chop the onion. Halve the leek lengthwise, wash
thoroughly and slice; wash and slice the celery.
Heat the oil in a pan and fry the onion, stirring
constantly. Add the chicken pieces and fry on
both sides. Put in the vegetables and pour on the
hot chicken stock, cover and simmer over a
medium heat for 45 minutes. Take out the chicken
pieces and remove the bones. Return the chicken

to the sauce and add the grated lemon peel; mix
well and heat thoroughly once more. Check the
seasoning, and before serving sprinkle on the
coconut flakes.

Dip the vegetable moulds in warm water, turn
out on to a plate and serve with the curry.

Chicken in spring sauce

1 tablespoon oil
4 chicken joints
450 ml/¾ pint chicken stock
salt and pepper
20 g/¾ oz butter
3 tablespoons mixed fresh chopped herbs or
1 tablespoon dried (parsley, chives, chervil)
1 tablespoon plain flour
1 tablespoon tomato purée
pinch of onion or celery salt
pinch of dried tarragon
5 tablespoons single cream

Heat the oil in a pan and fry the chicken joints
quickly on all sides. Pour on the hot stock with
seasoning to taste, cover and simmer over a
medium heat for 30 to 40 minutes. Melt the butter
in a small pan and fry the fresh herbs quickly,
stirring continuously, and mix in the flour and
tomato purée. Gradually stir in the cooking liquid
from the chicken, add the onion or celery salt,
tarragon and dried herbs if used and bring to the
boil. Add the chicken to the sauce and reheat
gently. Just before serving, stir in the cream and
adjust the seasoning.

Serve with: Rice or boiled potatoes and chicory
and orange salad

Chicken curry with chilled vegetable moulds

Braised chicken with vegetables

1 (900-g/2-lb) chicken
½ teaspoon salt
generous pinch pepper
1 teaspoon paprika pepper
100 g/4 oz streaky bacon, derinded
2 onions
1 tablespoon oil
450 ml/¾ pint hot chicken stock
250 g/8 oz mushrooms
350 g/12 oz frozen peas
3 tomatoes
4 tablespoons chopped parsley

If using a frozen chicken, place in a covered dish and thaw for at least 12 hours at room temperature. Remove the giblets from the chicken. Rinse it inside and out with cold water and sprinkle the inside with the salt, pepper and paprika. Chop the bacon; peel and chop the onions. Heat the oil in a large pan and fry the bacon, then brown the chicken on all sides with the onion. Pour on the hot stock, cover and simmer for 40 minutes. Add the mushrooms together with the peas and continue to cook over a low heat for a further 15 minutes. Cut the tomatoes at one end, cover with boiling water and leave for a minute, then peel and cut into small pieces and add to the chicken. Check the seasoning and continue to simmer for a short time, then take out the chicken, divide into portions, and arrange them on a plate with the vegetables. Garnish with parsley.

Poulet au citron

1 (900-g/2-lb) roasting chicken or 4 small chicken joints
2 tablespoons oil
250 ml/8 fl oz hot chicken stock
1 orange
100 ml/4 fl oz white wine
grated rind of 1 lemon
generous pinch of pepper
1 teaspoon concentrated curry paste
150 ml/5 fl oz soured cream

If using a frozen chicken, place in a covered dish and thaw at room temperature for at least 12

hours, or until completely thawed. Remove the giblets and wipe the chicken inside and out. Joint the chicken and dry well. Heat the oil in a pan and fry the chicken pieces thoroughly, then pour the stock over the chicken, cover and simmer for 45 minutes. Peel the orange and divide into segments, removing the pips and membranes as you go. Take out the cooked chicken and remove the bones, cutting the flesh into medium pieces. Add the white wine to the cooking liquid and stir in the grated lemon rind, pieces of orange, pepper and curry paste. Bring to the boil, then return the chicken to the stock and reheat thoroughly. Add the soured cream, check the seasoning and adjust to taste.

Serve with: Rice or mashed potato and green salad

Chicken and shrimp rice

1 (1.25-kg/2¾-lb) chicken
1 leek
475 ml/16 fl oz chicken stock
225 g/8 oz rice
125 g/4 oz mushrooms
150 g/5 oz shrimps or prawns, canned or thawed
150 g/5 oz frozen peas
salt and pepper

Joint the chicken into 8 pieces. Halve the leek lengthwise, wash thoroughly and chop. Bring the stock to the boil, put in the chicken pieces and leek, then cover and simmer over a medium heat for 30 minutes. Take out the chicken and after removing the bones, cut into medium pieces and return the meat to the pan. Wash and drain the rice, add it to the chicken and cook for a further 20 minutes. Wipe and slice the mushrooms thinly; drain, rinse and separate the shrimps. Ten minutes before the end of the cooking time add the mushrooms, shrimps and peas to the chicken. Adjust the seasoning before serving.

Chicken and shrimp rice; variation of Country-style chicken soup (page 8)

Turkey escalopes

4 turkey escalopes (each about 100 g/4 oz)
1 tablespoon plain flour
150 g/5 oz mushrooms
1 small onion
2 tomatoes
1 tablespoon oil
25 g/1 oz butter
generous pinch of salt and pepper
generous pinch of paprika pepper
generous pinch of dried oregano or marjoram

Coat the turkey escalopes with flour. Clean or peel the mushrooms and slice thinly; peel and chop the onion. Cut the tomatoes at one end, cover with boiling water and leave for a minute, then peel and cut into pieces. Heat the oil in a pan and fry the turkey escalopes on each side over a medium heat for 5 minutes. Transfer them to a warmed serving dish and keep hot. Add the butter to the remaining fat and fry the onion until soft. Add the mushrooms and tomato and season with salt, pepper, paprika and oregano or marjoram; cover and cook for several minutes. Arrange the cooked vegetables over the turkey escalopes and serve.

Serve with: Parsley potatoes and a green salad

Venison stew with aubergines

4 aubergines
1 onion
500 g/1 lb venison
1 tablespoon oil
2 tablespoons tomato purée
475 ml/16 fl oz chicken stock
salt and pepper to taste
1 teaspoon dried rosemary
2 tablespoons chopped parsley

Halve the aubergines, scoop out and chop the flesh, discarding the skins. Peel and chop the onion. Remove any membrane and sinew from the venison and cut into equal pieces. Heat the oil in a pan and fry the onion until soft, stirring continuously. Add the tomato purée, then mix the pieces of venison with the onion and tomato purée and fry for several minutes, stirring constantly. Pour over the stock with the seasoning and rosemary, add the aubergine, then cover and cook over a medium heat for 40 to 45 minutes. Adjust the seasoning to taste and garnish with parsley before serving.

Serve with: Dumplings or boiled potatoes

Spicy hare stew

250 ml/8 fl oz vinegar
475 ml/16 fl oz water
675 g/1½ lb hare or rabbit joints
1 bay leaf
3 peppercorns
8 tomatoes
1 large onion
1 clove garlic
3 tablespoons oil
½ teaspoon paprika pepper
250 ml/8 fl oz red wine
½ teaspoon salt
¼ teaspoon pepper
4 tablespoons chopped parsley

Mix the vinegar with half the water, pour over the meat, add the bay leaf and peppercorns, then cover and leave to marinate overnight in the refrigerator. Drain the meat but keep the marinating liquid. Cut the tomatoes at one end, cover with boiling water and leave for a minute. Peel and chop the onion. Peel and chop the garlic and crush with the blade of a knife. Peel and chop the tomatoes.

Heat 2 tablespoons of the oil in a pan and brown the meat completely, turning constantly. Season the meat with the paprika, add the tomato, garlic, 100 ml/4 fl oz of the marinating liquid, 250 ml/8 fl oz water and the red wine. Cover and simmer gently for 90 minutes. Heat the rest of the oil in a pan and fry the onion until golden brown. Remove the stew from the heat, add salt and pepper to taste, scatter over the onion and garnish with the parsley.

Serve with: Rice or pasta

Casseroled rabbit

(Illustrated below)

375 ml/13 fl oz red wine
2 small onions
2 bay leaves
4 cloves garlic, peeled and halved
1 carrot
½ leek
2 sticks celery
2 medium pieces rabbit (together about
675 g/1½ lb)
4 tablespoons oil
250 ml/8 fl oz chicken or beef stock
1 tablespoon cornflour
generous pinch each of salt and pepper
150 ml/5 fl oz single cream

Pour the red wine into a pan. Peel the onions and cut into eight, then add them with the bay leaves and garlic cloves to the wine. Scrape, wash and cut the carrot. Halve the leek lengthwise, wash thoroughly and chop; wash the celery and cut into pieces. Add all the vegetables to the wine and bring to the boil. Place the rabbit joints in a bowl and pour over the boiling liquid; sprinkle on 2 tablespoons oil, cover, allow to cool and marinate for 24 hours in the refrigerator.

Take the meat out of the marinating liquid, pat dry and rub with salt and pepper. Heat the remaining 2 tablespoons oil in a pan and fry the hare or rabbit quickly on all sides until well browned. Add the herbs and vegetables from the marinating liquid and brown, stirring continuously. Strain the rest of the marinating liquid, adding 250 ml/8 fl oz to the pan plus 250 ml/8 fl oz chicken or beef stock. Cover and simmer over a low heat for about an hour. Remove the meat from the stock, strain the liquid and return it to the pan. Mix the cornflour with a little cold water to form a smooth paste, pour into the stock and bring to the boil, stirring constantly. Return the rabbit to the sauce, adjust the seasoning, cover and simmer gently for a further 20 minutes. Stir in the cream before serving.

Serve with: Large field mushrooms or chanterelles, peeled pear halves filled with red cranberries, and flat noodles or dumplings.

Suitable for freezing: If intended for freezing, do not add the cream until the dish has been thawed again and thoroughly reheated. The gravy may need further thickening.

Vegetables and salads

Baked leeks

1 kg/2 lb leeks
40 g/1½ oz butter
4 tablespoons water
½ teaspoon salt
2 tomatoes
100 g/4 oz cooked ham
50 g/2 oz grated cheese

Remove the outside leaves and trim the ends from the leeks. Wash thoroughly in cold water and halve any long ones. Grease a soufflé dish with a little of the butter. Melt the rest in a pan, fry the leeks on all sides, add the water and salt, then cover lightly and simmer gently for 20 minutes. Cut the tomatoes at one end, cover with boiling water and leave for a minute, then peel. Cut the tomatoes and the ham into strips. Preheat the oven to hot (220 C, 425 F, Gas Mark 7). Place the cooked leeks with any remaining liquid in the ovenproof dish, place the ham and tomatoes on top and sprinkle with the cheese. Bake in the oven for 15 minutes.

Braised fennel

575 g/1¼ lb fennel (approximately 3 heads)
50 g/2 oz butter or margarine
salt and freshly ground black pepper
100 ml/4 fl oz white wine
25 g/1 oz butter

Remove the outer leaves of the fennel and cut off the root end. Wash, halve and slice. Melt the butter or margarine in a pan and fry the fennel quickly on all sides, stirring constantly. Add the seasoning, pour over the white wine, cover and simmer over a low heat for 30 minutes. Dot with butter before serving.

Vegetable casserole

1 small cauliflower
1 dash vinegar
4 eggs
300 g/12 oz frozen peas
1 (283-g/10-oz) can baby carrots
1 (241-g/8½-oz) can asparagus spears
20 g/¾ oz butter
2 teaspoons flour
300 ml/10 fl oz chicken stock
½ teaspoon salt
¼ teaspoon pepper

Soak the cauliflower, stalk upwards, for 20 minutes in water with a dash of vinegar added. Divide into florets, place in a pan, cover with boiling water and simmer gently until the florets are just cooked. Hard boil the eggs. Cook the peas following the directions on the packet. Strain the carrots and asparagus spears and keep the liquid. Towards the end of the cooking time, add the carrots and asparagus to the peas and heat very slowly.

Cool the eggs, shell and cut each into eight. Strain the cooked cauliflower and add it to the strained mixed vegetables. Melt the butter in a pan, add the flour and cook for 1 minute. Gradually add the stock, stirring continuously, and bring to the boil. Season to taste, then stir in the vegetables. Arrange in a heated dish and garnish with the egg.

Serve with: Lightly cooked meat, meatballs, baked, grilled or fried fish, pancakes or omelettes

Vegetable casserole

Creamed winter cabbage

1 Savoy cabbage (about 800 g/1¾ lb)
1 onion
½ teaspoon salt
3 tablespoons oil
2 teaspoons caraway seeds
¼ teaspoon pepper
1 teaspoon cornflour
4 tablespoons single cream

Remove the outside leaves of the cabbage, cut it into four, wash thoroughly, drain and shred. Peel and finely chop the onion. Place the cabbage in a pan with the salt, just cover with water and simmer over a low heat for 3 to 5 minutes. Strain the cabbage, keeping 150 ml/¼ pint of the cooking water. Heat the oil in a pan and fry the onion. Add the cabbage, caraway, pepper and the reserved cooking liquid, cover and simmer over a low heat for a further 10 minutes. Mix the cornflour with a little cold water until smooth, stir into the cabbage and, continuing to stir, bring to the boil. Add the cream and check the seasoning before serving.

Braised cabbage with horseradish

1 white cabbage (about 1-kg/2-lb)
2 onions
40 g/1½ oz butter
2 teaspoons sugar
1 teaspoon salt
¼ teaspoon pepper
2 tablespoons lemon juice
150 ml/5 fl oz chicken stock
1 tablespoon grated horseradish or horseradish cream
4 tablespoons chopped parsley
2 tablespoons natural yoghurt

Wash the cabbage, cut into four, remove the stalk and shred finely. Peel and chop the onions. Heat the butter in a pan and fry the onion, stirring continuously. Put in the shredded cabbage and fry lightly. Add the sugar, salt, pepper, lemon juice and stock, then cover and simmer gently for 20 minutes. Mix together the horseradish, parsley and yoghurt and stir into the cooked cabbage. Serve immediately.

Apple and carrot salad

2 apples
3 carrots (about 350 g/12 oz)
1 tablespoon lemon juice
½ teaspoon sugar
½ teaspoon salt
200 ml/7 fl oz single cream

Peel the apples; wash and scrape the carrots. Coarsely grate the apples and carrots and sprinkle with lemon juice. Stir the sugar and the salt into the cream and mix with the grated apple and carrot.

Mushroom salad with peppers

1 red pepper
2 tablespoons hot water
½ teaspoon salt
350 g/12 oz mushrooms
pinch of pepper
pinch of paprika pepper
4 tablespoons chopped parsley
3 tablespoons oil
2 tablespoons wine vinegar

Halve the pepper, remove the seeds and cut into thin slices. Simmer the pepper slices in the hot water with the salt for 5 minutes over a low heat in a covered pan; drain and cool. Wipe or peel and thinly slice the mushrooms. Mix together the pepper slices, mushrooms, cooking liquid, seasoning, paprika, parsley, oil and wine vinegar. Leave the salad for several minutes for the flavours to mingle, tossing occasionally.

Continental salad (page 56); Mushroom salad with peppers

Continental salad

(Illustrated on page 55)

2 eggs
1 head of lettuce
2 green peppers
1 cucumber
1 (283-g/10-oz) can asparagus spears
3 tablespoons oil
2 tablespoons wine vinegar
2 tablespoons apple juice
$\frac{1}{2}$ teaspoon salt
$\frac{1}{4}$ teaspoon pepper
pinch of celery salt
pinch of garlic powder
2 tablespoons fresh chopped or 2 teaspoons
dried mixed herbs (parsley, chives, chervil and
dill)

Hard boil the eggs. Remove the stalk and outside leaves of the lettuce and cut up or tear any large leaves. Wash under cold running water and drain well. Cut the peppers into rings and remove the seeds. Wipe and slice the cucumber thinly and drain the asparagus. Shake together the oil, wine vinegar, apple juice, salt, pepper, celery salt and garlic powder in a screw-topped jar until well mixed. Cool the eggs, peel and cut each into eight pieces. Mix the lettuce, pepper rings, cucumber and asparagus with the herbs and dressing and garnish with the egg.

Kohlrabi salad

3 kohlrabi globes
4 tablespoons chopped parsley
$\frac{1}{2}$ teaspoon salt
$\frac{3}{4}$ cup hot water
1 tablespoon wine vinegar
2 tablespoons oil

Peel the kohlrabi, remove the woody stem and cut into cubes. Wash, drain and chop the small, delicate green leaves of the kohlrabi and add to the parsley. Set aside. Simmer the kohlrabi with the salt and water in a small covered pan for 10 minutes, then leave the vegetable to cool in the liquid before draining. Beat together the parsley with the wine vinegar and oil, mix into the kohlrabi and serve.

Three summer salads

Lettuce with herbs

2 small heads of lettuce
$\frac{1}{2}$ teaspoon salt
$\frac{1}{4}$ teaspoon sugar
pinch of pepper
pinch of garlic powder
2 tablespoons cider vinegar
3 tablespoons oil
2 tablespoons fresh chopped or 2 teaspoons
dried mixed herbs (parsley, chives, borage, dill,
chervil and tarragon)

Remove the stalk and outer leaves of the lettuce. Cut up the leaves and remove any thick veins. Wash the leaves under cold running water and dry thoroughly. Beat together the salt, sugar, pepper and garlic powder with the cider vinegar and oil and, shortly before serving, mix into the lettuce with the herbs.

Tomato salad

6 large tomatoes
2 onions
$\frac{1}{2}$ teaspoon salt
$\frac{1}{4}$ teaspoon pepper
generous pinch of dried thyme
generous pinch of dried basil
1 tablespoon lemon juice or white wine vinegar
2 tablespoons oil

Wash and dry the tomatoes and cut into equal slices. Peel and finely chop the onions. Arrange the tomato slices on a plate and sprinkle with the onion. Shake together in a screw-topped jar the salt, pepper, thyme, basil, lemon juice or wine vinegar and oil and pour over the salad.

Farmhouse cucumber salad

1 large cucumber
1 teaspoon salt
pinch of dried basil
150 ml/5 fl oz soured cream

Slice the cucumber thinly and sprinkle with the salt. Leave in a colander for 20 minutes, then dry on absorbent kitchen paper. Stir the basil into the soured cream and dot over the cucumber.

Chicory and orange salad

(Illustrated on page 42)

3 heads of chicory
2 oranges
1 teaspoon sugar
$\frac{1}{2}$ teaspoon salt
$\frac{1}{4}$ teaspoon mustard
1 (150-g/5-oz) carton natural yoghurt

Remove any damaged outer leaves and the core from the root end of the chicory. Cut into slices, wash and drain. Peel the oranges thinly and separate the segments, removing the pips and membranes. Sprinkle with sugar and mix with the chicory leaves. Mix together the salt, mustard and yoghurt, stir into the salad and serve.

Three summer salads: Lettuce with herbs, Tomato salad and Farmhouse cucumber salad

Flemish salad

4 eggs
1 apple
3 heads of chicory
juice of $\frac{1}{2}$ lemon
2 small gherkins
4 tablespoons natural yoghurt
4 tablespoons single cream
2 tablespoons vinegar
$\frac{1}{4}$ teaspoon salt
$\frac{1}{2}$ teaspoon cream of horseradish
$\frac{1}{2}$ teaspoon sugar
300 g/11 oz cooked ham, shredded

Hard boil the eggs. Peel and quarter the apple, remove the core and cut into slices. Wash and shred the chicory; discard the core at the root end. Mix with the apple slices and sprinkle with the lemon juice. Chop the gherkins. Mix the yoghurt with the cream, vinegar, salt, horseradish and sugar, add the ham and gherkins and stir the mixture into the chicory and apple. Cool the eggs, peel and cut each into eight pieces. Arrange the salad in a dish and garnish with the pieces of egg.

Sauerkraut fruit salad

(Illustrated below)

450 g/1 lb canned or bottled sauerkraut
1 dessert apple
2 slices pineapple, canned in natural juice
5 tablespoons canned pineapple juice
10 cocktail cherries
4 tablespoons preserved red cranberries
1 tablespoon cider vinegar

Separate the sauerkraut with two forks. Peel and quarter the apple, remove the core and slice thinly. Cut the pineapple slices into small pieces. Mix the sauerkraut with the apple, pineapple, pineapple juice and the cocktail cherries. Mix the cranberries with the cider vinegar and stir into the salad.

Frankfurter salad

8 Frankfurter sausages
1 onion
1 pickled cucumber
1 (198-g/7-oz) can sweet corn
1 (70-g/2¾-oz) can pimientos
2 tablespoons oil
1 tablespoon wine vinegar
pinch of dry mustard
salt and pepper

Slice the sausages thinly. Peel and chop the onion and chop the pickled cucumber. Drain the sweet corn and mix with the Frankfurters, onion and cucumber. Drain the pimientos, slice them and mix into the salad. Whisk together the oil, wine vinegar, mustard and seasoning and pour the dressing over the salad.

Serve with: Toasted white bread or wholemeal bread

Egg salad with cheese dressing

4 eggs
3 tomatoes
1 pickled cucumber
1 dessert apple
200 g/7 oz cooked tongue, chopped
100 g/4 oz curd or sieved cottage cheese
1 tablespoon mayonnaise
½ teaspoon lemon juice
pinch of dry mustard
pinch each of salt and pepper
pinch of sugar
2 tablespoons milk

Hard boil the eggs. Wash, dry and cut the tomatoes into eight, removing the cores. Slice the pickled cucumber. Peel and quarter the apple, remove the core, and slice each quarter. Cut the tongue into strips. Cool the eggs, shell and cut each into eight. Beat together the cheese, mayonnaise, lemon juice, mustard, salt, pepper, sugar and milk and carefully mix this dressing into the salad.

Serve with: Wheaten rolls

Ham and asparagus salad

(Illustrated above)

500 g/1 lb asparagus, fresh or canned
½ teaspoon salt
2 eggs
1 lettuce
200 g/7 oz cooked ham
2 tablespoons chopped fresh mixed herbs or
parsley
pinch each of salt and pepper
1 tablespoon wine or cider vinegar
3 tablespoons oil
2 tablespoons apple juice

Trim the fresh asparagus and remove the woody part of the stem or if canned, just drain. Cut into 5-cm/2-inch pieces. Put the fresh asparagus into a pan with salted water, cover and cook for 15 to 25 minutes. Hard boil the eggs.

Trim the stem and remove any wilted outside leaves from the lettuce, tear up any large leaves and wash and dry well. Cool and shell the eggs and cut the ham into equal strips. Drain the cooked asparagus and leave to cool. Halve the eggs and remove the yolks. Mash the yolks with a fork and mix in the chopped herbs, salt, pepper, vinegar, oil and apple juice. Chop the egg whites. Mix the lettuce leaves with the asparagus and strips of ham and pour on the dressing. Sprinkle over the chopped egg white before serving.

Serve with: Wholemeal bread and butter

Italian pasta salad

1.5 litres/2¾ pints water
1 teaspoon cooking salt
200 g/7 oz short spaghetti or macaroni
200 g/7 oz cooked ham
1 (190-g/6¾-oz) can pimientos
2 gherkins
4 tablespoons oil
2 tablespoons wine vinegar
½ teaspoon mustard
¼ teaspoon salt
generous pinch of black pepper
4 tablespoons chopped parsley

Bring the water to the boil, add the salt, put in the spaghetti or macaroni and cook for 15 minutes. Cut the ham, pimientos and gherkins into strips. Drain the spaghetti, rinse with boiling water and drain again before mixing with the ham, pimiento and gherkin. Whisk together the oil, vinegar, mustard, salt and pepper and toss into the salad. Cover and leave until cool. Toss well, garnish with parsley and serve.

Trieste noodles

(Illustrated below)

2 litres/3½ pints salted water
250 g/9 oz flat noodles
1 (225-g/8-oz) can peach slices
4 gherkins
1 (184-g/6½-oz) can pimientos
4 tablespoons chopped parsley
1 (250-g/9-oz) can mussels
pinch each of salt and pepper, dried sage and dried rosemary
1 tablespoon wine vinegar
2 tablespoons oil

Bring the salted water to the boil, put in the noodles and boil for about 15 minutes. When cooked, drain the noodles and rinse with cold water. Drain and chop the peaches and slice the gherkins and pimientos. Mix all the ingredients together with the seasoning and herbs. Shake together the vinegar and oil and pour it over the noodle mixture; mix in well and allow to marinate for several minutes.

Beef and tomato bake

10 tomatoes
2 onions
350 g/12 oz minced beef
1 egg
½ teaspoon salt
¼ teaspoon pepper
generous pinch of paprika pepper
generous pinch of celery salt
40 g/1½ oz butter or margarine
300 g/12 oz cooked rice
4 tablespoons chopped parsley
2 tablespoons grated cheese
2 tablespoons fresh breadcrumbs

Cut the tomatoes at one end, cover with boiling water and leave for a minute. Peel and cut the tomatoes into pieces; peel and chop the onions. Mix together the minced meat with the onion, egg, salt, pepper, paprika and celery salt. Grease an ovenproof dish with a little of the butter or margarine, place a layer of rice at the bottom then half the tomato pieces, next the mince mixture and a layer of chopped parsley, then another layer of rice and finally a layer of tomato. Mix together the cheese and breadcrumbs and sprinkle over the tomato. Dot with the remaining butter or margarine and bake for 1 hour in a moderately hot oven (190 C, 375 F, Gas Mark 5).

Serve with: Mushroom salad with paprika

Corned beef bake

(Illustrated on page 62)

250 g/8 oz potatoes
½ head celery
½ teaspoon salt
2 generous pinches of grated nutmeg
300 ml/10 fl oz milk
20 g/¾ oz butter or margarine
1 tablespoon plain flour
generous pinch of pepper
400 g/14 oz corned beef

Peel the potatoes, cut into small pieces and boil in a little water until soft. Wash the celery well, scrape and dice, then boil for 15 minutes until soft in a little salted water. Mash the cooked potato and mix well with the salt, grated nutmeg and 1 to 2 tablespoons hot milk. Melt the butter or margarine in a pan, stir in the flour and cook for 2 minutes over a low heat, stirring continuously. Gradually stir in the rest of the milk and bring to the boil. Add the celery with its cooking liquid to the sauce and return to the boil once more. Season with a pinch of nutmeg and pepper.

Using a fork, break the corned beef into pieces. Grease an ovenproof dish with a little extra butter or margarine, place half the potato in the bottom, then add the corned beef. Cover with the sauce and finish off with the rest of the potato. Cook for 20 minutes in a moderately hot oven (200 C, 400 F, Gas Mark 6).

Serve with: Green salad

Potato and sausage goulash

250 g/9 oz pork sausagemeat
2 onions
2 green peppers
2 tablespoons oil
1 tablespoon tomato purée
2 teaspoons paprika pepper
600 ml/1 pint chicken stock
800 g/1¾ lb potatoes
salt and pepper
4 tablespoons chopped chives

Divide the sausagemeat into equal pieces and form into balls. Peel and chop the onions. Halve seed and slice the peppers. Heat the oil in a pan and fry the onion and pepper, stirring constantly. Mix in the tomato purée and paprika, add the sausagemeat balls and stock; cover and cook over a medium heat. Peel and dice the potatoes. Add to the pan with the seasoning, cover and cook for a further 20 minutes. Before serving sprinkle with the chives.

Serve with: Tomato salad

Mushroom and potato pie

2 large onions
2 green peppers
4 tomatoes
2 tablespoons oil
250 ml/8 fl oz chicken stock
salt and pepper
pinch of paprika pepper
pinch of dried marjoram
500 g/1 lb mushrooms, fresh or canned
1 packet mashed potato or 450 g/1 lb cooked
potato, mashed with
125 to 250 ml/5 to 8 fl oz milk
pinch of grated nutmeg
40 g/1½ oz butter or margarine
4 tablespoons chopped parsley
2 tablespoons fresh breadcrumbs

Peel the onions and cut into rings. Halve, seed and slice the peppers. Cover the tomatoes with boiling water and leave for a minute, then peel and cut into pieces. Heat the oil in a pan and fry the onion rings and peppers for several minutes, stirring constantly. Add the tomato and the stock; season with salt, pepper, paprika and marjoram, cover and simmer for 10 minutes. Drain the mushrooms if canned, wipe or peel and chop coarsely if fresh, add to the vegetables, cover and continue cooking. Prepare the instant potato according to the instructions on the packet; season the potato with salt, pepper and grated nutmeg. Preheat the oven to moderately hot (200 C, 400 F, Gas Mark 6). Grease an ovenproof dish with a little of the butter or margarine. Place a layer of potato in the dish, add the vegetables, sprinkle on the parsley, cover with the remaining potato and finally sprinkle with the breadcrumbs. Dot with the remaining butter or margarine. Cook for 15 minutes.

Serve with: Veal cutlets or liver fried in a little fat and green salad

Opposite page: Corned beef bake (page 61). *Below:* Mushroom and potato pie

Leek hotpot

100 g / 4 oz streaky bacon
2 onions
225 g / 8 oz lean boneless pork
1 tablespoon oil
250 ml / 8 fl oz chicken stock
½ teaspoon salt
generous pinch pepper
500 g / 1 lb potatoes
500 g / 1 lb leeks
2 tablespoons single cream

Remove the rind and dice the bacon; peel and chop the onions. Wipe the pork, remove any membranes and sinews. Trim away any remaining fat and cut into 2.5-cm/1-inch pieces. Heat the oil in a pan and fry the bacon, then add the onion and pork and continue to fry, stirring constantly. When the meat is lightly browned pour in the stock, add salt and pepper, cover and simmer for 20 minutes. Peel and cut the potatoes into pieces and add to the meat. Halve the leeks lengthwise, remove the ends and wash thoroughly. Cut into 3-cm/1-inch pieces and add to the meat and potatoes with a further 100 ml/4 fl oz water. Stir well, cover and cook for another 30 minutes over a low heat. Before serving take off the heat, adjust the seasoning, and stir in the cream.

Ham and rice soufflé

300 g / 12 oz brown rice
2 litres / 3½ pints water
½ teaspoon salt
200 g / 7 oz lean ham
3 eggs
2 tablespoons chopped parsley
¼ teaspoon salt
pinch of pepper
pinch of grated nutmeg
2 tablespoons oil

Wash the rice and drain. Bring the water with the salt to the boil, add rice and simmer over a low heat for 30 to 40 minutes. Cut the ham into thin strips. Separate the eggs and beat the yolks with the parsley, salt, pepper and nutmeg. Whisk the egg whites until stiff. Grease an ovenproof dish with 1 tablespoon of oil. Mix the cooked rice with the ham, egg yolk mixture, 1 tablespoon of oil and finally fold in the egg whites. Place the mixture in the greased dish and bake in a moderately hot (200 C, 400 F, Gas Mark 6) oven for 20 minutes.

Serve with: Tomato sauce or ketchup

Chicory gratin

(Illustrated on page 67)

575 g / 1¼ lb heads of chicory
300 g / 11 oz cooked ham
pinch each of salt and pepper
1 teaspoon lemon juice
50 g / 2 oz butter or margarine
1 tablespoon Parmesan cheese

Remove any damaged outer leaves of the chicory and the core from the root end. Wash the heads and shred. Cut the ham into strips and mix with the chicory, salt, pepper and lemon juice. Grease an ovenproof dish with a little of the butter or margarine. Place the chicory and ham in the dish and dot with the rest of the butter or margarine, cover and bake in a moderately hot (200 C, 400 F, Gas Mark 6) oven for 20 minutes. Ten minutes before the end of the baking time take off the cover and sprinkle on the grated Parmesan cheese.

Serve with: French bread or mashed potato

Leek hotpot

Bacon risotto

225 g/8 oz smoked streaky bacon
1 large onion
1 red or green pepper
3 tablespoons olive oil
1 clove garlic, crushed
generous pinch of salt
225 g/8 oz long-grain rice
225 g/8 oz white cabbage
2 tablespoons concentrated tomato purée
750 ml/1¼ pints chicken stock
100 g/4 oz frozen peas
4 Frankfurter sausages
freshly ground black pepper

Remove the rind and roughly chop the bacon. Peel and chop the onion. Remove the seeds and pith from the pepper and cut the flesh into small dice. Place the bacon in a large heavy-based frying pan or saucepan and cook it slowly until the fat runs. Remove the bacon from the pan and drain it on absorbent kitchen paper. Add the olive oil to the pan together with the garlic, onion and pepper. Season with a pinch of salt and cook the mixture, stirring frequently, for 2 to 3 minutes. Stir in the rice and continue to cook for 5 minutes or until the grains are beginning to brown. Stir the mixture continuously to prevent it from burning.

Shred the cabbage and add to the pan together with the tomato purée, then carefully pour over the stock and bring it to the boil. Add the frozen peas and reduce the temperature. Simmer the risotto over low heat for 10 minutes. Meanwhile, slice the Frankfurters and stir them into the half-cooked rice mixture. Cook gently for approximately 10 minutes longer or until most of the stock is absorbed and the risotto is just moist. Finally, stir in the cooked bacon and season the dish with a little freshly ground black pepper.

Serve with: Tomato salad (page 56) or Farmhouse cucumber salad (page 56) and French bread.

Suitable for freezing: If it is intended for freezing, do not add the cabbage and frozen peas. Before serving the defrosted risotto, melt 50 g/2 oz butter in a large frying pan and add the finely shredded cabbage and peas. Cook, stirring continuously, for 10 minutes then add the risotto, reduce the heat and cover the pan. Leave over very low heat until thoroughly reheated.

Stuffed peppers

225 g/8 oz rice
1 litre/1¾ pints water
½ teaspoon salt
1 onion
400 g/14 oz pork luncheon meat
1 tablespoon oil
4 large green peppers
1 (198-g/7-oz) can sweet corn
350 g/12 oz frozen peas
salt and pepper
250 ml/8 fl oz meat stock

Wash and drain the rice. Bring the water to the boil with the salt, add the rice and simmer over a low heat for 20 minutes. Peel and finely chop the onion. Cut the luncheon meat into cubes. Heat the oil in a pan and fry the onion, stirring constantly. Cut off the tops of the peppers and remove the seeds. Drain the sweet corn and separate the frozen peas, running them under cold water, if necessary. Mix together the meat, onion, sweet corn and frozen peas with the seasoning. Rinse the cooked rice briefly in cold water, drain and add it to the meat, peas and sweet corn mixture. Fill the peppers with this mixture, replace the tops and stand the peppers upright in a large saucepan or flameproof casserole. Pour over the stock, seasoned to taste, cover and simmer over a low heat for 25 minutes.

Serve with: French bread or wholemeal bread and butter

Opposite page: Chicory gratin (page 65)

Cauliflower cheese with ham

1 large cauliflower
1 dash vinegar
1 teaspoon salt
200 g/4 oz cooked ham
40 g/1½ oz butter or margarine
2 tablespoons plain flour
600 ml/1 pint milk
1 egg yolk
1 teaspoon lemon juice
pinch each of salt and pepper
4 tablespoons grated cheese

Remove the outer leaves and stalk of the cauliflower and soak for 20 minutes in vinegar water, florets downwards. Drain and cook in boiling salted water for 20 minutes. Cut the ham into strips. Take out the cauliflower and drain. Melt the butter or margarine, sprinkle in the flour and cook, stirring continuously, for 1 minute. Gradually add the milk and, stirring constantly, bring the sauce to the boil. After a few minutes, remove from the heat and stir in the egg yolk, lemon juice and ham and season to taste. Place the cauliflower in a deep ovenproof dish, pour on the sauce, sprinkle with cheese and brown under the grill.

Savoury beef pancakes

(Illustrated on page 26)

FOR THE FILLING
100 g/4 oz cooked beef
1 onion
1 gherkin
1 tablespoon capers
1 tablespoon oil
1 tablespoon flour
3 tablespoons single cream
½ teaspoon salt
generous pinch of pepper
2 tablespoons chopped parsley
FOR THE PANCAKES
50 g/2 oz plain flour
¼ teaspoon salt
1 egg
150 ml/5 fl oz milk
2 tablespoons oil

Mince the beef. Peel and chop the onion, chop the gherkin and halve any large capers. Heat the oil and fry the onion until soft. Add the capers, gherkin and the minced beef and reheat thoroughly, stirring constantly. Sprinkle the flour over the meat and cook, stirring continuously, for 2 to 3 minutes, then stir in the cream and heat gently until thickened. Add the seasoning, mix in the parsley and remove from the heat.

To make the pancakes, sift the flour and salt into a bowl, make a hollow in the centre and break the egg into this. Mix together the flour and egg and gradually add the milk, beating until the mixture is smooth. Heat the oil in a frying pan and cook four thin pancakes one after the other. Fill each pancake with meat mixture and roll up.

Stuffed tomatoes

1 egg
1 onion
1 bunch chives
4 large lettuce leaves
150 g/5 oz continental sausage
100 g/4 oz cheese, sliced
1 gherkin
1 dessert apple
8 medium tomatoes
2 tablespoons mayonnaise
2 tablespoons curd or sieved cottage cheese
2 tablespoons single cream
pinch each of salt and pepper
pinch of paprika pepper

Hard boil the egg. Peel and chop the onion, wash, dry and snip the chives. Wash and dry the lettuce leaves and place one on each of four plates. Cut the sausage and the cheese into thin strips, and the gherkin into small dice. Peel and quarter the apple, remove the core and cut the flesh into small pieces. Wash and dry the tomatoes, cut off the stalk end, scoop out the centres, discarding the seeds, and reserve the pulp. Cool, then shell and chop the hard-boiled egg. Mix the tomato pulp with the chopped egg, apple, gherkin, cheese, sausage, onion and chives. Beat the mayonnaise with the curd or sieved cottage cheese and cream, and season with salt, pepper and paprika. Stir this dressing into the salad. Pile the stuffing into the tomato shells and set two on each lettuce leaf.

Serve with: Wholemeal bread and butter

Savoury mushroom pancakes

(Illustrated above)

100 g/4 oz self-raising flour
4 eggs
150 ml/¼ pint milk
pinch of salt
1 onion
400 g/14 oz mushrooms
4 tablespoons oil
4 tomatoes
salt and pepper
pinch of chopped fresh or dried thyme
4 tablespoons chopped parsley

To make the pancake batter, sift the flour into a mixing bowl, make a hollow in the centre and break in the eggs. Mix thoroughly, then gradually add the milk and a pinch of salt and beat until smooth. Alternatively, a blender can be used to mix the batter. Leave to stand for a few minutes for the starch grains to swell.

Peel and chop the onion, wipe or peel and chop the mushrooms. Heat 2 tablespoons of the oil in a pan and fry the onion until soft, stirring constantly to prevent it browning. Add the chopped mushrooms, cover and cook gently over a low heat for about 5 minutes. Wipe and quarter the tomatoes and add them to the mushrooms. Season with salt, pepper and thyme.

Heat a little of the remaining oil in a frying pan, pour in a quarter of the batter mixture and cook until set, then turn and brown the pancake on the other side. Remove from the pan and keep warm until the rest of the batter and oil have been used to make three more pancakes. Add the parsley to the mushroom mixture, top each pancake with some filling, fold and serve.

Serve with: A green salad

Three milk cocktails

Melon milk

For each glass:
150 ml/¼ pint milk, well chilled
4 tablespoons melon pulp
½ teaspoon sugar
1 teaspoon maple syrup

Liquidise the milk, melon pulp, sugar and syrup in a blender and serve with a straw.

Cucumber milk

For each glass:
150 ml/¼ pint milk, well chilled
4 tablespoons grated cucumber
pinch each of salt and pepper

Liquidise the milk, grated cucumber, salt and pepper in a blender and serve very chilled.

Tomato milk

For each glass:
4 tablespoons single cream
2 teaspoons concentrated tomato purée
1 teaspoon lemon juice
generous pinch of salt
150 ml/¼ pint milk, well chilled

Stir the cream into the tomato purée, add the lemon juice and sprinkle in the salt. Gradually stir in the milk. If preferred, double cream can be used instead of single. In this case, whip it until stiff, then spoon it on top of the tomato milk cocktail.

Clockwise from the left: Melon milk, tomato milk and cucumber milk

Egg and shrimp savoury

(Illustrated on page 15)

1 (200-g/7-oz) can shrimps or prawns
1 onion
20 g/¾ oz butter
½ teaspoon paprika pepper
2 tablespoons oil
4 eggs
4 large lettuce leaves
4 slices brown bread
salt and freshly ground black pepper
4 tomatoes (optional)
4 sprigs dill or parsley (optional)

Drain and separate the shrimps or prawns. Peel and chop the onion. Heat the butter in a small pan and fry the onion. Add the shrimps and paprika, cover and cook over a low heat.

Heat the oil in a frying pan and fry the eggs. Wash the lettuce leaves, dry and place one on each slice of bread. Spoon the shrimp and onion over the lettuce leaves and place an egg on top of each. Season well. Wipe, quarter and arrange the tomatoes. Garnish with dill or parsley.

Eggs in herb sauce

4 eggs
40 g/1½ oz butter or margarine
2 tablespoons plain flour
250 ml/8 fl oz milk
250 ml/8 fl oz chicken stock
2 egg yolks
generous pinch of salt
2 tablespoons chopped fresh herbs or 2
teaspoons dried mixed herbs

Hard boil the eggs. Melt the butter or margarine in a pan, add the flour and cook for a minute over a low heat, stirring constantly. Gradually add the milk and stock, stirring all the time, then bring slowly to the boil, lower the heat and simmer gently for 10 minutes. Beat the egg yolks with the salt and stir in a little of the hot sauce. Remove the pan from the heat and stir the egg yolk mixture into the sauce. Sprinkle in the herbs and keep the sauce warm, without letting it boil. Shell the eggs, halve, and place in the sauce for serving.

Florentine toasts

(Illustrated above)

4 eggs
500 g/generous 1 lb leaf spinach, fresh or frozen
½ teaspoon salt
pinch of pepper
pinch of grated nutmeg
40 g/1½ oz butter or margarine
8 small slices white bread
4 tablespoons single cream
6 tablespoons grated cheese
½ teaspoon paprika pepper

Hard boil the eggs, cool and shell. Wash fresh spinach well, put in a pan with only the water that clings to the leaves, cover and cook over a low heat for about 8 minutes, or until just tender. If frozen, follow directions on the packet. Drain off as much liquid as possible, then stir the salt, pepper, grated nutmeg and butter or margarine into the spinach, cover and cook for a further 10 minutes. Toast the slices of bread on both sides and preheat the grill to its hottest. Divide the spinach between the slices of bread, halve the eggs lengthways and place on the spinach, cut sides down. Mix the cream with the cheese and paprika and use to top the egg halves and spinach. Heat under the grill until the cheese begins to brown.

Gourmet desserts

Blackcurrant sponge pudding

(Illustrated on page 74)

225 g/8 oz blackcurrants
2 peaches
1 teaspoon cornflour
3 tablespoons cold water
1 tablespoon brown sugar
100 g/4 oz plain flour
1½ teaspoons baking powder
pinch of salt
2 tablespoons sugar
50 g/2 oz butter
100 ml/4 fl oz milk

Wash and drain the blackcurrants, Skin the peaches, remove the stones and slice thinly. Mix the cornflour to a smooth cream with the cold water, stir in the brown sugar and put in a pan with the fruit. Cover and cook over a low heat for 7 minutes. Mix the flour with the baking powder, pinch of salt and the sugar. Melt the butter and, adding the milk, beat it into the flour to form a smooth paste. Place the fruit in an ovenproof dish, pour over the flour mixture and bake in a moderately hot (200 C, 400 F, Gas Mark 6) oven for 20 to 25 minutes until golden. Serve while still warm, with single cream, if liked.

This pudding can also be made with canned bilberries, in which case the fruit should be well drained. Other berried fruits are also suitable.

Raspberry apples

250 g/9 oz fresh raspberries
2 tablespoons sugar
few drops vanilla essence
4 cooking apples
1 tablespoon honey
100 g/4 oz chopped almonds, toasted
1 teaspoon grated pistachio nuts

Keeping back a few, place the raspberries in a pan with a tightly fitting lid, together with the sugar, vanilla essence and 3 tablespoons of water and stew over a low heat for up to 5 minutes, stirring from time to time. Peel the apples, cut about a third off the tops to form lids and remove the cores from the centre. Strain the raspberries, returning the liquid to the pan. Put the apples in the pan, cover and simmer over a low heat for 10 minutes. Stir the honey into the liquid to form a thin syrup, and coat the outside of the apples. Roll the coated apples in the almond flakes and press on the coating, then fill the hollowed-out apples with the raspberries, top with the fresh ones and sprinkle over with the pistachio nuts.

Blackcurrant and peach cobbler

(Illustrated on cover)

225 g/8 oz plain flour
2½ teaspoons baking powder
40 g/1½ oz butter or margarine
50 g/2 oz castor sugar
150 ml/¼ pint milk
FOR THE FILLING
1 (411-g/14½-oz) can peach slices
450 g/1 lb fresh or frozen blackcurrants
50 g/2 oz granulated sugar
a little beaten egg

For the scone topping, sift the flour with the baking powder and rub in the butter until the mixture resembles fine breadcrumbs. Stir in the sugar followed by the milk to form a soft dough. Knead lightly on a floured board and set aside for 10 to 15 minutes.

For the filling, drain the peaches reserving 4 tablespoons of juice, mix the fruit with the sugar, and place in an ovenproof dish.

Roll out the scone dough to 1 cm/½ inch thick, cut into circles with a small pastry cutter and arrange over the fruit. Glaze with beaten egg and bake in a hot oven (220 C, 425 F, Gas Mark 7) for 10 minutes. Reduce to moderate (180 C, 350 F, Gas Mark 4) and bake for a further 20 minutes.

Serve with: Custard or whipped cream

Left: Blackcurrant sponge pudding (page 73).
Below: Baked gooseberry custard

Lemon cream dessert

2 lemons
2 eggs
4 tablespoons castor sugar
few drops vanilla essence
450 ml/¾ pint milk
3 tablespoons hot water
20 g/¾ oz gelatine

Wipe the lemons, finely grate the peel and squeeze out the juice. Separate the eggs. Whisk the egg yolks with the grated lemon peel, lemon juice, sugar and the vanilla essence until creamy. Warm the milk. Put the hot water in a bowl and stand the bowl in a pan of boiling water. Sprinkle in the gelatine and stir until dissolved, then stir the dissolved gelatine into the milk. Gradually add the milk to the egg yolk mixture and leave until half set. Whisk the egg whites until stiff and fold them into the setting cream. Leave to finish setting in the refrigerator for about 2 hours. Serve on the same day.

Baked gooseberry custard

3 dry bread rolls
250 ml/8 fl oz milk
2 eggs
75 g/3 oz castor sugar
500 g/1 lb fresh ripe or frozen gooseberries
2 tablespoons butter or margarine
4 tablespoons single cream

Slice the rolls thinly. Heat the milk and when lukewarm, pour over the rolls. Whisk the eggs with the sugar until creamy and mix with the rolls. Preheat the oven to moderate (180 C, 350 F, Gas Mark 4). Pick over, wash and drain the gooseberries. Grease an ovenproof dish with a little of the butter or margarine, mix the drained gooseberries with the bread mixture and spoon into the dish. Stir in the cream and dot with the remaining butter or margarine. Bake for 40 to 45 minutes, until set and lightly browned.

This pudding can also be made with grapes.

Strawberry cream dessert.

Strawberry cream dessert

500 g / 1 lb fresh strawberries
1 tablespoon lemon juice
3 tablespoons hot water
15 g / ½ oz gelatine
3 egg yolks
100 g / 14 oz castor sugar
250 ml / 8 fl oz milk
250 ml / 8 fl oz double cream

Hull the strawberries, crush with a fork and sprinkle with the lemon juice. Sieve the strawberries, cover the pulp and place to one side. Put the hot water in a bowl and stand it in a pan of boiling water. Sprinkle with gelatine and stir until dissolved.

Whisk the egg yolks with the sugar in a bowl until frothy. Warm the milk and gradually add to the egg and sugar mixture. Place the bowl over a saucepan of hot water and whisk until the mixture begins to thicken, but do not overcook or the sauce will curdle. Remove it from the heat, stir in the dissolved gelatine and mix with the strawberry pulp. Beat the cream until stiff and fold into the pudding. Leave to set in the refrigerator.

Fruit cup with chocolate sauce

300 g / 11 oz cottage cheese
1 tablespoon sugar
1 teaspoon lemon juice
2 peaches
225 g / 8 oz cherries
100 g / 4 oz plain chocolate

Beat the cottage cheese with the sugar and lemon juice. Immerse the peaches for a short time in hot water, divide in half, peel, stone and slice thinly. Wash and stone the cherries. Mix the peaches and cherries with the cottage cheese. Melt the chocolate in a basin over a pan of hot water and pour over the dessert.

Index